PROFILES OF VALOR

4

Character Studies
from the
War of Independence

Marilyn Boyer &
Grace Tumas Ehrman

Master Books First Printing: November 2025

Master Books® is a division of the
New Leaf Publishing Group, LLC.

ISBN: 978-1-68344-428-2
ISBN: 978-1-61458-947-1 (digital)

All Scripture verses are from the King James Version of the Bible.

Please consider requesting that a copy of this volume be purchased by your local library system.

Printed in the United States of America

Please visit our website for other great titles:
www.masterbooks.com

For information regarding promotional opportunities, please contact the publicity department at pr@nlpg.com.

Character Studies
from the
War of Independence

January 1781 – February 1832

Credits

Thanks to the following people for their investment in helping to preserve these inspiring stories from America's past. It is my prayer that their efforts will reap a bountiful harvest as these stories will serve to be an inspiration to those in whose hands America's future lies!

I wish to thank David Barton, who has been such an inspiration to me, personally, to become excited about learning about our godly heritage. God has gifted him for such a time as this in our country. He is the master of primary source documents! Tuesday night has traditionally been "Barton night" in our home as we gather to watch his DVDs and invite friends in to learn with us! It is only as we get truth back into the public square that we can hope to preserve the heritage of freedom handed down to us.

Thanks to Grace Tumas Ehrman, for her role in crafting these stories in such a way that they are a delight to read! It's great when even the editors have to read the stories first to see what happens and then go back and edit!

Thanks to my dear friend Mary Ann Edman who is the world's most efficient multi-tasker, committed to producing quality that will be a tribute to our

Lord and Savior. Her creativity has been indispensable in producing the layout and graphic design for this book as well as editing the mistakes the rest of us overlooked!

Thanks to Judy Saunders, my long-time friend and prayer warrior, for her faithful work in the tedious editing process. God has gifted her with a precise eye for detail. She sees things I just don't notice. Thanks, my friend!

Thanks to my son, Rick, who, despite his incredibly busy life, has read these stories to his children at night, while editing each for accuracy of content to assure we are portraying these men and women in an worthy manner, giving honor where honor is due.

Chronological Table of Contents

Table of Contents by Character Quality

Introduction

The founding era of our country is crucial to understand since the foundations of our Christian heritage were laid during this time, and today most of us do not know enough about this to defend the fact that we were once a Christian nation. This does not mean that everyone living then was a Christian but that Christian principles formed the basis of our government and influenced the policies society implemented. It was Christianity that shaped the foundations on which our country was established. Even non-Christians or deists, such as Benjamin Franklin and Thomas Jefferson, held a high regard for biblical standards.

Confusion reigned in the Continental Congress while trying to agree on whether to use the Articles of Confederation or write a new Constitution to govern our country. Benjamin Franklin spoke up to acknowledge that God governs in the affairs of men. He reminded the men that except the Lord build the house, they labor in vain. He then called the delegates to prayer to seek direction from God.

Thomas Jefferson established the Bible as the main textbook in Washington, D.C. schools while president of the United States. Inscribed on the Jefferson Memorial are Jefferson's affirming words, "God who gave us life gave us liberty. And can the liberties of a nation be thought secure when we have removed their only firm basis, a conviction in the minds of the people that these liberties are the Gift of God? That they are not to be violated but with His wrath? Indeed, I tremble for my country when I reflect that God is just; that His justice cannot sleep forever." He believed the Bible to be of great benefit to those who read it and applied its teaching to their lives. He contributed from his own funds to have copies of the words of Jesus printed and distributed to Native American tribes.

Alexis de Tocqueville, in 1831, was sent to America by Louis Phillipe of France to discover what made America great, in hopes to help his strife-torn nation. His conclusion after 18 months of study and observation was this: "I sought for the greatness and genius of America in her commodious harbors and her ample rivers—and it was not there. ... In her fertile fields and boundless forests—and it was not there ... in her rich mines and her vast world commerce—and it was not there ... in her democratic Congress and her matchless Constitution—and it was not there. It was not until I went into the churches of America and heard her pulpits flame with righteousness did I understand the secret of her genius and power. America is great because she is so good, and if America ever ceases to be good, she will cease to be great."[1] What he observed was a desire on the part of imperfect people inspired by the spiritual revival of the Great Awakening to acknowledge God and to seek to follow Him daily with their lives. May the example set by these patriots serve as impetus to us today to lay aside selfish pursuits and live lives wholly dedicated to the Lord. I pray that God will use each of you to make a positive difference in your sphere of influence as each of these patriots did in their day.

Marilyn Boyer

Cautiousness

DEFINITION

Knowing how important right timing is in accomplishing a task

MEMORY VERSE

In all thy ways acknowledge him, and he shall direct thy paths.
Proverbs 3:6

Double Agent

James Armistead

Yorktown, Virginia
1781

He could smell smoke from British campfires as he strolled through the camp. Horses whinnied softly and groups of chatting Redcoats clustered around the gun carriages. Thirty-three-year-old James Armistead glanced sharply around him as he walked close by General Charles Cornwallis' headquarters. His tattered, earth-colored slave clothes and his story gave him a passport to this British camp. Posing as a slave escaping from the

American patriots, the young Black man had easily found work as an orderly and guide.

James Armistead Lafayette

Richmond, Virginia, lay in chaos and ashes after the British torched it. Looters prowled the streets, breaking into houses and stealing property. The Virginia Legislature piled into carriages and leaped onto horseback, and galloped out of the city. Benedict Arnold's turncoats lurked everywhere. They looked like patriots, but they bled British colors. By 1781, the focus of the war had switched to the south, where colonists fought for their lives in the mountains, swamps, farmlands, and cities of Virginia, Georgia, and South Carolina.

The young aristocratic French general, Marquis de Lafayette, decided to throw in his men with the

American cause against British General Charles Cornwallis. In order to do this, he began recruiting spies from all walks of life and sending them undercover behind British lines. One of these, a slave named James Armistead, obtained permission from his master to assist the patriots and volunteered as a spy. Unlike many spies who simply located information and carried it back to their side, Armistead assumed the dangerous role of a double agent.

First, he infiltrated the British service as an orderly in Benedict Arnold's camp. Arnold commanded one of the two British armies in the Richmond area. Cornwallis headed the other. Hundreds of escaped slaves came over to the Redcoats during the course of the war in return for their promised freedom. Assuming the role of an escaped slave, no one noticed anything unusual about Armistead. The spy ambled through the British lines, his quick dark eyes noting the number of cannons and the troop positions. He did not write anything down just then. His razor-sharp mind recorded the information and filed it away until he could record it. Going about his business as an orderly near Cornwallis' camp, he often came near groups of soldiers on duty. He listened when they spoke about the war. He wanted to know how they felt about it. Did they think they were winning? Or did they secretly fear the Americans? He put his finger on the pulse of the British Army's morale and counted its heartbeat.

He totaled up the average number of soldiers on the move.

Armistead moved as cautiously as a cat. In the officers' quarters, lit by candlelight, he moved among the tables, bowing his head deferentially like an obedient servant. Generals sipped tea from fine bone china teacups. They put their heads together to discuss plans, objectives, and attacks. They spoke freely, argued, boasted. They looked right through him. Armistead could have smiled to himself. Nobody paid attention to an escaped slave unless they wanted to march with a guide through dense thickets without fear of a colonist shooting them in the back from behind a tree.

During the day, Armistead served as a guide, piloting British troops safely through the countryside. But at night, he turned into something entirely different. Like a wolf, he slipped out of the officers' tent. Once, he bumped into another Black servant. Whispering in his ear, James Armistead disappeared into the darkness. The other Black man slipped through British lines that night to pass the information on to General Lafayette. Able to read and write, Armistead usually wrote his reports down just before he smuggled them out through other American spies. Satisfied with Armistead's loyalty, Arnold and Cornwallis used him as a spy. While he tapped their resources for information, he also fed them disinformation: inaccurate data that never found its way back to its source. He found it risky but easy to fool Cornwallis. With American help,

The Marquis de Lafayette with James Armistead

Armistead forged a large order for new colonial recruits. Then Armistead appeared at Cornwallis' headquarters with a dirty piece of paper he claimed he had found crumpled in the road. Cornwallis, reading the request for additional troops, believed that the Americans outnumbered him. None of the other spies that Lafayette sent behind British lines could tell him anything until he began receiving Armistead's precise information on August 31, 1781. This news enabled Lafayette to spring an attack on British forces, trapping them at Hampton.

One day, as he travelled unobtrusively through the countryside between the American lines and British headquarters, Armistead saw signs of massive numbers of troops on the move. The British navy began landing ten thousand British soldiers in the vicinity of Yorktown. Armistead knew that this meant that the British had a major operation in the wings. Quickly, he passed on his detailed information to Lafayette, who in turn, relayed it to Washington. Washington could not believe his luck. Washington knew if he moved quickly, he could trap the British in Yorktown—the place Cornwallis had planned as his center for operations. Because Armistead moved fast and provided accurate data, Washington quickly laid siege to Yorktown and prevented the crucial ten thousand reinforcements from reaching their goal. With Rochambeau's French fleet blocking escape routes by sea and the Continental Army blockading the British from outside, the siege of Yorktown proved to be the last major battle of the war. When the exhausted British finally surrendered on October 19, 1781, General

Lafayette acknowledged that Armistead's work as a double agent had proved instrumental in securing the American victory.

Cornwallis did not appear at the official surrender. But as he later visited with Lafayette in the Frenchman's headquarters, the British general looked up with shock to see Armistead, whom he had thought of as his personal spy, wearing the buff-and-blue uniform of the Continental Army.

Following the war, James Armistead returned to his master. Under the Slave Act of 1783, he did not qualify to receive freedom because he had served as a spy, not a soldier. Two years later, when General Lafayette visited Armistead in Virginia, he was outraged to learn that Armistead was still a slave. The General immediately wrote a strong letter of recommendation to the Virginia Legislature. Armistead received his freedom in 1787. Demonstrating his gratitude and admiration for the man who had helped make this possible, the ex-slave changed his name to James Armistead Lafayette.

James Armistead demonstrated cautiousness in performing his mission in such a way as to not reveal his true allegiance, thereby greatly aiding the American cause of liberty!

This is to certify that the [James Armstead] has done essential services to me while I had the honour to command in this State. His Intelligence from the ennemy's [sic] camp were industriously collected and most faithfully delivered.

—Marquis de Lafayettee,
in a letter describing James Armstead's service as a spy

Questions

1. Give examples of how James Armistead practiced cautiousness.
2. Tell how Armistead put his own interests below that of his country.
3. How did doing his job well give him greater opportunity?
4. What "small jobs" do you have now? Remember, learning to do well in little things brings greater opportunities later.
5. Think of a time you were cautious in accomplishing a task.
6. How did Layfayette reward Armistead for his cautious and devoted service to his country?
7. Despite his work during the war, James Armistead returned to slavery after serving in a war meant to bring freedom to other Americans. How would that make you feel if you were James Armistead?

Decisiveness

DEFINITION

The ability to make wise, deliberate decisions based on God's standards

MEMORY VERSE

If any of you lack wisdom, let him ask of God, that giveth to all men liberally, and upbraideth not; and it shall be given him.

James 1:5

Cowpens

Gen. Daniel Morgan

Cowpens, South Carolina

January 17, 1781

They reached the swampy meadows called Hannah's Cowpens towards dark. Cows wandered through the empty pastures, stopping here and there to crop a mouthful of dead grass. After stumbling across the flooded Broad River, General Daniel Morgan and seven hundred Continental infantrymen settled on the damp ground for the night to await an impending British attack. Somewhere in the darkness behind them, the men imagined that they could hear the distant hoof-beats of "Bloody

Brigadier General Daniel Morgan

Tarleton's Legion" of redcoats. Sent south after the Battle of Camden in October, 1780, to report to General Nathanael Greene, Morgan had orders to cultivate local support and harass Lord Cornwallis' troops. At all costs, however, he was instructed to avoid a direct battle.

In December, Cornwallis learned of Morgan's mission. In response, he ordered twenty-six-year-old

Colonel Banastre Tarleton to head west to stop Morgan. Nicknamed "Bloody Tarleton," after he slaughtered American soldiers at Waxhaws when they surrendered, Tarleton swept out of camp at the head of his infamous Legion. Over one thousand light infantrymen and British cavalrymen galloped off into the South Carolina countryside. Christmas day found Morgan camped on the Pacolet River in the South Carolina backcountry.

Tarleton and his Legion of redcoats rode hard after Morgan. The wily frontiersman, realizing the pursuit, dodged Tarleton first at the town of Ninety-Six before temporarily losing him near the Broad River. Morgan and his patriots then headed north, maneuvering so as to avoid getting trapped in a pincer movement between Tarleton and Cornwallis. They had been on the run since then.

Tonight, Morgan discussed the options with his men. They could obey orders and continue to try to evade the enemy without being captured, or they could turn and engage the enemy in battle. The tall, rough general, clad in a frontiersmen's jacket, moved among the men huddled together. Despite his bad grammar, and his reputation as a tough fighter, Morgan had proved himself during Lord Dunmore's War against the Native Americans.

Morgan's face, grim in the ruddy light of the flames, bore the scar of a bullet that punched through his left jaw and knocked out his teeth. Now, as he walked among his men, he encouraged them and told them how he expected them to perform in the coming fight. Finally, he stripped off his shirt and turned his back to the men. White scars from four hundred and ninety-nine lashes crisscrossed his back—a reminder of his punishment twenty years before for punching a British officer in the face. Morgan decided to stand his ground against the British.

Anticipating the ensuing battle with the British, Morgan's men passed a brief, restless night. Tarleton and his troopers arrived at 3 a.m. on the morning of January 17th. Morgan was ready for him. Skillfully assessing his enemy, Morgan decided to use Tarleton's impatience and his scorn for the militiamen to his advantage. On the patriot side, Morgan could muster three hundred Continentals in addition to his experienced, but half-trained militiamen. Having already determined how Tarleton would act in a given situation, Morgan turned his attention to the topography, or the terrain.

In the chilly winter darkness, the American general deployed his men in three main defense lines, arranging the skirmishers at the top of a sloping hill out in front. These men had orders to fire two volleys and then retreat behind the safety of the second line. The next line, hidden just beyond the crest of the hill, would also fire twice. As they, in turn, retreated behind the Continentals, these regular troops would rise from a hollow about one hundred fifty yards behind them.

The British arrived in the confusing half-light of early dawn. Seeing the first line of Americans stretched along the high ground, Tarleton panicked, sending his men tumbling into battle before they had fully deployed. As several regiments of Tarleton's regulars plunged at the hill, Morgan's skirmishers kept their backs to them. Suddenly, they wheeled and fired at point-blank range into the Redcoats' faces. The longer range and accuracy of the Virginia riflemen knocked another rank of troopers to the

The Battle of Cowpens

ground. Then the skirmishers retreated quickly, leaving the British to face a fresh line of militiamen. The first two lines helped to slow Tarleton's advance. Struggling up the hill against a storm of bullets, the British regulars fought hard, engaging the Continental line in combat. Morgan, realizing that his militiamen would probably run while the Continentals took the hardest blow, placed General Andrew Pickens' reserved forces and William Washington's cavalry out of sight in a little hollow to the rear.

Meanwhile, Tarleton ordered his 71st Highlanders to advance and attempt to roll up the American right wing in a flanking movement. Bellowing hoarsely amid the smoke, Lieutenant Colonel John Eager Howard alerted his men with orders to face to the right. His men, however, mistook the order, and instead of outflanking Tarleton, the entire line began filing out in an orderly retreat. Seeing this, Morgan immediately turned the mistake to his advantage. Tarleton's attack, weakened by the uphill advance and confrontation with the skirmishers and then the militia, slowed down as it reached the top of the hill. Morgan ordered his third line, the Continentals, to retreat to a spot he pointed out and then open fire.

The British advance ground to a halt under the deluge of gunfire. At that moment, Morgan counterattacked with Washington's cavalry, crushing Tarleton's legion in a double envelopment. In less than an hour, Tarleton's Legion had been reduced to 136 men, totaling 110 killed and 800 captured, two hundred of those wounded. Banastre Tarleton escaped with his skin, while the patriots confiscated his equipment and supplies, and rounded up the officers' slaves. Cornwallis, faced with the loss of Tarleton's Legion, also had his light infantry obliterated, a loss which would cripple his ability to maneuver quickly for the remainder of the war.

The American victory at Cowpens proved the single greatest tactical victory of the war. By demonstrating decisiveness, Daniel Morgan executed the most successful double envelopment in modern military history, making the Battle of Cowpens a turning point in the Revolutionary War.

His strength and spirit, his frank and manly bearing, his intelligence and good-humor, set off by a rich fund of natural wit . . . rendered him a favorite among the people.

—James Graham,
biographer of Morgan

Questions

1. What was Morgan's mission and what was Cornwallis' response when he learned of it?
2. What kind of reputation did Colonel Tarleton have? Why?
3. Why did Morgan show his men his back?
4. What character flaw did Colonel Tarleton possess that General Morgan used to his advantage?
5. What battle plan did General Morgan devise?
6. What was the initial reaction of the Redcoats?
7. How did General Morgan decisively use Lieutenant Howard's mistake to his ultimate advantage?
8. What effect did the victory at Cowpens have on the war as a whole?
9. Think of someone in the Bible who acted with decisiveness in the midst of an adverse situation.
10. Think of an instance when you were unsure of what to do, but acted with decisiveness.

Purposefulness

DEFINITION

Exercising determination to stay the course until the goal is achieved

MEMORY VERSE

Without counsel purposes are disappointed: but in the multitude of counsellors they are established.

Proverbs 15:22

The Star Fort

Gen. Nathanael Greene

Ninety-Six, North Carolina
May 22–June 19, 1781

A wooden palisade, surrounded by a deep ditch, yawned at the hot South Carolina sky. Felled trees, with sharpened branches jutting out, encircled the fort, discouraging attackers from climbing over the wall. Inside the fort, Colonel John Cruger, an American Tory from New York, sat waiting with his men. Considered some of the finest soldiers in the Loyalist army, Cruger's troops included poor, rugged countrymen and crack marksmen from the Carolina backcountry. Discovering that American

General Nathanael Greene intended to attack this lonely outpost, Cruger quickly dug in. Thick, dark trees and tangled undergrowth surrounded the village of Ninety-Six with its twelve houses, a courthouse, and a "sturdy jail." A covered ramp ran down from the jail to the Branch Spring nearby, the fort's only water source. Almost a hundred people lived near the fortified town. Cleared land stretched for half a mile around. The hot, treacherous backcountry smothered the rest of the landscape in silence. With Nathanael Greene only days away, Cruger prepared for a siege by building several

Lt. Colonel John Cruger

blockhouses inside the fort, and constructing a portable gun platform. His artillerymen rolled several brass three-pounder field guns onto the five salient or star-shaped platforms and aimed their muzzles out at the darkening woods. They lay quietly, waiting for the first patriot troops to appear at the fringe of the trees.

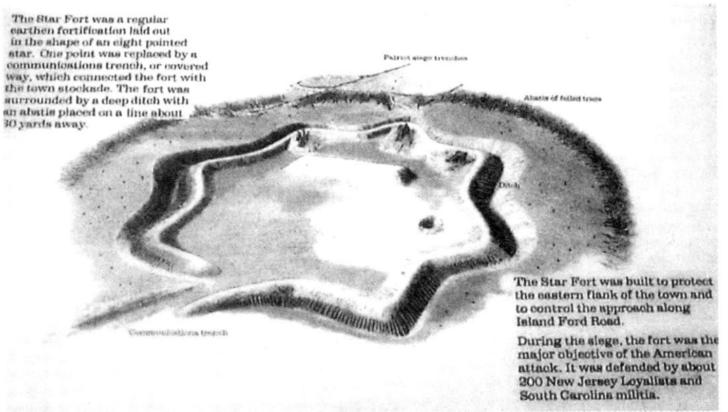

The Star Fort

After the Battle of Guilford Court House, Lord Charles Cornwallis licked his victorious wounds while thirty-nine-year-old General Nathanael Greene led his men on a tactical retreat. Entering the war as a militia private, Greene rose quickly through the ranks to major general in the Continental Army. Following Horatio Gates' defeat at Camden, Washington placed Greene in command of the

Southern Army. Putting his purposeful generalship to the test, he allowed Cornwallis to invade Virginia. Meanwhile, Greene swung around to seize the South Carolina backcountry from British hands and force the redcoats to evacuate the colony. Probably Washington's most skilled general, Greene purposefully divided his enemy, eluded them on back roads, and exhausted the British in their attempts to locate them. While the British defeated him in every single battle during the Southern campaign,

Count Thaddeus Kosciusko

Greene forced them to pay for these temporary victories with heavy casualties. Following a Loyalist uprising in 1775, the patriots crushed Tory resistance in the Carolinas. Despite this defeat, bitter feelings would simmer in the backcountry for the rest of the Revolutionary War.

Abandoning Camden in May 1781, Francis, Lord Rawdon ordered British Colonel John Cruger to evacuate his post at Ninety-Six, North Carolina, and head towards Savannah, Georgia. Ninety-Six served as the lynchpin in a chain of Loyalist forts strung through the southern backcountry. As long as the British could control these forts, they held nominal control over the region. Only days before, General Andrew Pickens' men intercepted Rawdon's message to Cruger and informed Greene. After May 15, 1781, the only British outposts remaining in the high country stood at Ninety-Six in South Carolina and Augusta, in Georgia. Besides these two defenses, the British only held Charleston, two hundred miles southeast on the coast. Sending Andrew Pickens and Colonel Henry Lee to take Fort Augusta, Greene moved to attack Cruger's isolated outpost at Ninety-Six.

Greene set off at once for Ninety-Six, arriving on May 22nd. Camping in four spots around the fort, Greene felt his spirits sink as he viewed the strong fortifications. Finally, after talking with his Polish engineer, Count Thaddeus Kosciusko,

Maham Tower

Greene decided to open the siege with nine hundred seventy-four troops. Kosciusko advised Greene to concentrate the bulk of his troops against strongest point of defense, the Star Fort. The Polish engineer laid out the siege lines in traditional European fashion. Then he instructed his men to begin digging trenches in order to safely approach the fort. Unfortunately, he began burrowing too close to the redoubt. As the men began digging only seventy yards away from the fort, Cruger's men unleashed a barrage of cannon and musket fire. The patriots scrambled from the trenches and retreated to a distance some two hundred yards away. They began again on the other side of a wide, dark ravine. Kosciusko, bustling about, ordered the men to build two earthen cannon batteries three hundred fifty yards to the north of the Star Fort.

The rocky soil, baked hard as iron by the sun, made the digging more difficult. Finally, they finished the first angle or parallel of the trench on May 27th. Once they had penetrated the ground, the next parallel only took three days. As they crept nearer to the fort, Cruger's men increased their fire to a constant barrage. Next, the patriots pushed a mine under the fort wall. Alerted to the danger, Cruger's men raced out to prevent the mine from exploding. During the brief, fierce fight, Kosciusko fell with a bayonet wound. With only seventy yards left to go to reach the Star Fort, Kosciusko had his men chop down trees to build a wooden Maham Tower about thirty feet in the air. Then they constructed a wooden platform with a roof at the top of the tower. Crouching under this cover, the patriot marksmen could fire straight over the wall into the Star Fort. Each time they pulled a trigger, another of Cruger's artillerymen went down.

Attack on the Star Fort

Cruger immediately countered the problem of the Maham tower by dragging sandbags to the walls in order to make the parapet three feet higher. Now his sharpshooters, lying under cover, could fire through loopholes left between the sandbags. Still, the Americans in the tower posed a grave threat to the fort. The resourceful colonel poured heated shot into his cannon muzzles and fired, landing the balls on the tower's roof in an attempt to set the shingles on fire. But the green logs would not burn.

Greene's men countered Cruger's fire-ball tactics with their own measures. While Cruger hopelessly aimed cannonballs at the Maham Tower, the Americans sent flaming arrows whizzing into the fort, hoping to set the wooden structure alight. As fiery arrows rained down at them from the tower, Cruger desperately tore the roofs off the buildings to keep them from catching on fire. The two sides lay watching each other from behind their trenches and sandbags. Wind, heat, and rain beat down on Cruger's men inside the roofless fort, while Greene's troops alternately shivered or roasted.

Bullets rained down on the open fort all day. As the sun set, Cruger moved his artillery platform out of shelter and opened fire on the American lines. He used this barrage to distract Greene's sharpshooters while a small party of thirty men from DeLancey's Brigade slipped out of the fort. Lieutenant John Roney led them towards the enemy trench. Groping in the darkness, they came up against several men from a trench-working crew. During the fight, two or three Americans fell to the ground. Moving softly towards the trench, the British officer and his men scraped the dirt back into the ditch. As they emerged, they caught sight of several slaves carrying entrenching tools. Gunfire broke out as the British marched their few prisoners back to the fort. Suddenly, a bullet struck Lieutenant Roney's body. He crumpled to the ground, mortally wounded, in the darkness.

After the small British mission sallied forth, Greene made a second attempt to burn out the defenders in the Star Fort. That day, heavy grey clouds overspread the sky, giving the darkening woods and sharp, palisade walls a gloomy air. They ordered Sergeant Whaling, with ten men from the Legion, to take armloads of "incendiary materials," run up under the walls of the fort, and set the bundles on fire. Whaling understood that he was going on a suicide mission. Carefully buttoning his coat, he said goodbye to his friends. Then he rolled into the enemy trench. An alarm sounded as he landed. As the men tried to set fire to the fort, the Loyalists attacked them savagely. Four men staggered back, all except one wounded. Sergeant Whaling died in the ditch at the fort. His enlistment would have been up in two days.

At this point, Greene sent a message to Cruger, demanding his surrender. Huddled inside the fort, with only a few men wounded, the British colonel saw no reason to give up.

Colonel Lee came up from Augusta, Georgia, on June 8th, after taking the fort there. His men immediately began digging siege trenches in the hard ground in front of Holmes Fort. This redoubt guarded the water source at Spring Branch as well as the western side of the town. Meanwhile, moving along the third parallel, Kosciusko began tunneling under the parapet of the Star redoubt. By rolling several barrels of gunpowder into the tunnel and positioning them below the parapet, Kosciusko hoped to blast a large hole in the earthworks. Greene's men worked day and night. They regularly rotated shifts with some men standing guard while others ate and slept, and the rest patiently scraped at the earth and hauled away rocks. Worried by the tunnels that moved ever closer to the fort, British troops slipped out of the fort at night. Under cover of darkness, these men attacked lonely guards standing on duty near the siege-works. Others hastened to throw the dirt back into the trenches. Once in a while, the British managed to capture a stash of entrenching tools. In spite of these setbacks, the patriots continued digging the trenches until they came to within a few feet of the fort.

Upon his arrival, Lee shifted his cannon to overlook the Spring Branch creek. Up to this point, the British could slip out of the fort to get water from the spring. Now, cut off from his only water supply, Cruger tried to dig a well inside the Star Fort. After digging for some time, they failed to reach the water table. Each time a soldier raised his head from either the wall or the trenches a sharpshooter on the opposite side drew a bead on him. Despite raging thirst, the garrison held out grimly.

Meanwhile, the Carolina backcountry buzzed with the news that Francis, Lord Rawdon, hearing about the garrison's plight, had undertaken a forced march from Charleston with over two thousand Irish troops on June 7th. Several days later, a young local woman decided to try to get Rawdon's message through to the Loyalists trapped in the fort. Although both her father and brother served in the patriot army, the girl was in love with a Tory officer. Since her marriage to him, the ties that bound her to his cause proved stronger than anything else. Hearing about Lord Rawdon's approach, she whispered the word to a young Loyalist boy that day at a nearby farmhouse. Swinging up onto his horse, the boy galloped off towards Ninety-Six. As he rode into the stockade, the American sharpshooters grabbed their muskets. The boy raced on, under crackling fire from the patriot pickets and snipers. Encouraged by cheers from the men inside the fort, the boy ducked through the gate with news of Rawdon's relief party.

At noon the next day, Greene learned about Rawdon's approach from his own spies in Charleston. Greene knew that if he did not capture Ninety-Six by the time Rawdon came, then the British would force him to retreat without his prize. With time running out, Greene sent General Francis Marion, the "Swamp Fox" to locate Rawdon and slow him down. For some reason, Marion and his men could not march fast enough either to catch or distract Rawdon. Worried, because his men had not finished the tunnel necessary to blow up the parapet, Greene decided to attack the fort quickly and purposefully. On June 18th, both sides prepared for battle. Greene intended to stage a simultaneous attack on the Star Fort and Holmes Fort.

The five points of the star battery glared down at the Americans as Lieutenant Duval, at the head of his Maryland troops, faced the British three-pounder guns. Lieutenant Seldon, commanding the First Virginians, poised to lead the shock troops in the first wave of attack.

Behind them, a group of men shouldered their pole-hooks. Over on the American right, Major Randolph's infantry and Captain Kirkwood's Delaware Regiment steadily held their ground. Facing the deadly quiet fort with its black loop-holes, the Americans moved under the cover of the

Major General Nathanael Greene

trenches until they came to within a few yards of the Loyalists' main ditch.

Near noon, a cannon blast shook the earth. At this signal, the artillery blazed out. Small-arms fire crackled from the trenches as the first unit tumbled into the fort's ditch under cover of the smoky haze. As the patriots leaped into the trench, Cruger's men met them with bristling bayonets. Musket-fire erupted from the slits between the sandbags as the star-shaped redoubt allowed Cruger's troops to sweep the area with gunfire. The first wave of men attacked the fort, fighting to secure the position, while the axe-men hooked their poles into the sandbags and hauled them down. As the sandbags tumbled into the ditch, backwoods marksmen in the Maham Tower fired into the exposed fort. At the same time, the crossfire from both sides of the fort cut two-thirds of the Americans down like grass. Both commanding officers lay mortally wounded on the hard ground. Cruger, seeing the sandbags pitching into the ditch, sent out two companies of Delancy's Loyalists to destroy the hook-men.

At the same cannon blast, Lee and his smaller party assaulted Fort Holmes, taking it easily. As Greene's troops chopped down the abatis, Cruger pulled his men together and launched a counterattack. His men struck with bayonets and clubbed muskets at the flanks of the American attackers. After a brief and bloody tussle in the trenches, lasting nearly three-quarters of an hour, Greene called his men back. They retreated under a hail of lead, dragging most of their wounded with them. Greene had suffered heavy casualties during the unsuccessful frontal assault. Looking around the battlefield, Greene called for a cease fire in order to let his men bury their dead and exchange prisoners. Colonel Cruger turned down his request. He knew that the side that won would dig the graves. The siege had lasted twenty-eight days—the longest siege of the war. The British had suffered twenty-seven killed and fifty-eight wounded. Greene experienced significantly higher casualties at fifty-eight dead, seventy wounded, and twenty missing. In addition, the patriot militia had lost more than fifty men. The next morning, with Rawdon only thirty miles away from the fort, Greene called a halt to the siege. He withdrew with his men northeast towards Charlotte, North Carolina.

As Greene retreated, the British realized that they could not afford to garrison the lonely outpost at Ninety-Six. Instead, they marched out into the compound, tore down the Star Fort, and set fire to the town. Billowing smoke and the smell of charred wood pursued Lord Rawdon on the long road away from Ninety-Six. Circling around, Greene and his troops harassed Rawdon through the sweltering South Carolina heat all the way back to Charleston. Rawdon's Irish troops, worn out by the long march and the hot sun, did not have the strength to chase.

Greene let his men rest for six weeks in the High Hills of the Santee. Then his army engaged the British for one last time outside of Charleston at Eutaw Springs on September 8, 1781. It would be the last major battle of the Southern campaign. Meanwhile, the British pulled their forces back to Charleston. They would remain isolated there for the rest of the war. Nathanael Greene's southern campaign forced the British to give up their strategy of occupying the Carolina backcountry.

Nathanael Greene demonstrated purposefulness by beginning the siege at Ninety-Six and taking the chance to attack the Star Fort, even if the assault proved unsuccessful. The southern campaign and the siege of Ninety-Six proved an important turning point in the Revolutionary War. From this point, as Cornwallis' invasion of Virginia ended with his surrender at Yorktown, the tide turned in America's favor.

Questions

1. Was the village of Ninety-Six large?
2. Why did General Greene purposely divide his army?
3. Why was Ninety-Six an important fort?
4. How did Greene's men approach the fort?
5. How did Greene's men manage to cut off the water supply from the fort?
6. Why did Greene feel he must attack the fort quickly?
7. How long did the siege last?
8. Why did the seige of Ninety-Six prove to be an important turning point in the war?
9. How did Nathaniel Greene demonstrate purposefulness in the way he led his men?

Availability

DEFINITION

Being willing to attend to a need
when I am called to help

MEMORY VERSE

Also I heard the voice of the Lord,
saying, Whom shall I send,
and who will go for us?
Then said I, Here am I; send me.
Isaiah 6:8

Ride Down the Moon

Emily Geiger

Saluda and Congaree Counties,
South Carolina
June 1781

Thick grey Spanish moss grew so low that it brushed against her face. It blocked the sun from the tunnels of live oaks, making it already twilight though the red sun still hung on the rim of the world. Cherokee Indians or Jesuit priests sometimes paddled deep into the swamp, to catch sight of a wildcat or build a stone chapel. But most of the settlers did not go far. There was something about the swamp that repelled intruders. Alligators' snouts, emerging like snags of submerged branches, floated gently on the surface of the water.

Everywhere hung the smell of rotting vegetation, the branches of the bald cypresses protruding from the still, dark water like bony fingers. Far above her head, they grew in a narrowing vortex, tapering thinner and thinner towards the forbidden sky. Eighteen-year-old Emily Geiger urged her horse faster. With the message hidden in her clothes, she could not go home tonight.

In the summer of 1781, General Nathanael P. Greene, retreating from an unsuccessful assault on the British at the fort at Ninety Six, struggled through the swampy bottomlands of the southern Carolinas. Pursued by Lord Rawdon, he had managed to put the Saluda and Enoree Rivers between him and the enemy. When they crossed the south side of the Enoree River, Rawdon fell back, unwilling to clash with Greene's superb cavalry led by Colonel Washington and Colonel Lee. Camped at the fork of the Enoree and Broad Rivers and cut off from any aid, Greene desperately needed to get a message through to General Thomas Sumter to join forces with him. But Sumter's camp lay one hundred miles away on the Wateree River, while Lord Rawdon, who had split his army in two, now blocked his way. There was little hope of getting around Lord Rawdon's camp to contact Sumter while the woods crawled with Tory spies.

Trapped and uncertain what to do, Greene waited with mounting anxiety as British forces in the area strengthened. The General kept looking for ways to get word out, but few messengers wanted to risk such a dangerous assignment. Finally, Greene determined to break out of the British encirclement.

General Nathanael Greene

On the morning planned for the move, Emily Geiger listened to the low murmurs in the other room as she worked around the farmhouse two miles from Greene's encampment. Her father, John Geiger, a German settler and a loyal patriot, lay painfully bedridden. A neighbor, who knew about the American army's desperate situation, had ridden over to explain the details. As Emily listened, a great plan swelled inside of her. When war broke out in the Carolinas, she had complained bitterly that she could not seize a gun and fight in place of her sick father. Now she had an opportunity to be useful. Without waiting another moment, she hurried down the road to Greene's encampment.

When she arrived at the general's headquarters, Greene sat in deep anxiety, pondering his next move. Just then, an orderly informed him that a young woman had arrived and wanted to see him.

"Let her come in," the General ordered.

Emily, walking inside with the officer, faced General Greene and told him of her plan. She told him that she would carry the message to General Sumter, since she had heard that he had found no one to do it for him. She told him that she could easily trace the route, since she had been that way to her Uncle John's house several times.

The General hesitated. He hated to send a young woman off alone into woods and swamps full of wild animals, hostile Native Americans, and Tory spies. He would never forgive himself if something happened to her. But she seemed able and determined to do the job, and he simply had no choice. Finally, Greene agreed to let her go. He sat down and wrote out a dispatch to Sumter. Then he went over it with Emily sentence by sentence, until she had memorized every word. This way, if the British captured her and she had to destroy the message, she could deliver it verbally to General Sumter.

Emily Geiger crossing the Saluda River

When Emily left Greene's camp, she rode into her own farmyard and swung down from her horse. Quickly, she flung the side-saddle over the best-blooded horse in the stable and tightened the girths. As she rode out, she did not notice a pair of sharp eyes watching her.

Lowry, Emily Geiger's close neighbor, watched as the dust rose and settled on the road. That girl was up to no good. Not even Lowry's closest neighbors suspected a man who refused to get involved in the war at all—on either side. They respected a man's conscience to sit tight in these times. It certainly did not hurt to feel the solid chink of British gold in your hand, either. Four hours later, a fellow spy in Greene's camp came to inform Lowry that Emily had gone to see the General. Now all Lowry had to do was send the man on to catch her.

Emily swam the Saluda River at Kennerly's Ferry, just above the junction on the Broad. Her tired legs bounced against the horse's sweating sides. As it began to grow dark, she knew that she had to stop and find a place to rest. No one should ride through these woods alone at night. When she finally came to a settlement, she gave the village a wide circle. Instead, she saw the light from a lonely cabin and knocked at the door. To avoid suspicion,

Emily riding to General Sumter's camp

Emily immediately told the people that she was trying to get to the house of a man named Ellwood who lived ten miles further on. Her Tory hosts did not bless the Continental Congress, but they knew John Geiger and respected him. They made Emily feel at home as they gave her something to eat and stabled her horse.

"Yes," exclaimed the wife warmly, "if you were the daughter of my worst enemy you should have food and shelter."

Emily settled down for the night with one ear open. Suddenly, she jerked awake to the sound of galloping hoof-beats. Outside, someone hallooed loudly. When the Tory family opened the door, a man stepped inside. Soft conversation floated around her. Emily only caught bits of it, but what she heard made her lie still. Lowry had sent a spy named Billy Mink to track her down. Mink, seeing Emily sound asleep, decided to bunk down and catch a few winks himself. He could always seize her before morning. Finally, talk died down like embers on the hearth. Softly, Emily rose, tiptoed to a window, and dropped quietly to the ground outside. A dog sprang at her, but she bent and stroked its head. It did not bark as she moved away. Moonlight shone brightly on the stables. Picking her way through the summer darkness, alive with the sudden chirring cry of night animals, Emily saddled her horse and crossed a nearby ploughed field to muffle the sound of hoof-beats.

Fear drove her like a whip. Nearby, white mist was rolling across the bottomlands. Fear lay in the fire-lit house beside the ploughed fields. Fear rode the high moon down the glimmering white road.

Her own words, bravely spoken to General Greene, pounded in her head. A woman can pass where a man cannot. She rode for hours, pushing her horse as hard as she could. She could hear the horse's breath shuddering in its nostrils as she clung to its damp neck. Shadows of owls, bobcat, deer, wild pigs, and coyotes danced through the trees. Then pink dawn approached and light showed through the trees. She had covered two-thirds of the one hundred miles to Sumter's camp. As she rode through the thick hardwoods towards Firday's Ferry on the broad, flat Congaree River, three of Lord Rawdon's Tory scouts burst out of the trees and surrounded her horse. Emily realized that they had seen her riding alone from the direction of General Greene's camp. They glanced at her horse's heaving flanks covered with white lather.

"Where are you going?" they demanded.

"I'm on my way to my Uncle Jacob's house," she told them. But her cheeks turned a bright rosy color.

The men glanced at her blushing face and then at each other. Something was wrong. They did not believe her. Suddenly, they came on either side of her, bringing her under arrest to Lord Rawdon at

Fort Granby a mile away. When Emily answered their questions evasively, the soldiers took her to a tiny room on the upper floor of the guardhouse and locked her in. The British knew that it went against all the rules of war and gallantry to search a woman spy themselves, but they had to find out if she carried a message. Someone hurried off to find a Tory matron.

Standing alone in the room, Emily thought fast. She must not lose her head. If they found a message hidden on her, she would probably be tried and hanged as a spy. There was no way she could possibly conceal it in this small room. A thorough search would certainly turn it up. If she threw the message out the window, a passing guard would find it. Suddenly, the answer came to her clear as her father's voice, as soft as a whisper of hope. She fumbled in her bodice for the message. Unfolding it, she scanned the memorized lines, searing them like flashes of lightning into her brain. Then she tore the paper into shreds and began to eat it. Choking, she gulped down the last bit just as the door opened.

The old Tory woman, Mrs. Hogabook, searched Emily from head to foot. Finally, Mrs. Hogabook stood up, her hands empty. She scolded Lord Rawdon's men for detaining and searching the girl, saying that she found no incriminating evidence. Emily refused to say anything. Ashamed, the officer commanding the British scouts apologized profusely and gave Emily an escort all the way to her uncle's home. She could not shake off the soldiers just then, but the next day, she set off on a roundabout trip. Finally, at three o'clock on the hot afternoon of the third day, she struck onto a travelled road. To her relief, she saw soldiers dressed in the uniform of the Continental Army marching along the dusty road. The men took Emily straight to General Sumter's camp on the Wateree River. Dusty, disheveled, and exhausted, Emily staggered in to see the General. After relating the story of her adventures, Emily rattled off the message verbatim from General Greene. The astonished General Sumter gathered his men together in an hour and made ready to march to the junction listed by General Greene. By receiving the dispatch, Sumter was able to come to Greene's aid and join up with the main army at Orangeburg. Two weeks later, Emily finally made it home to her farm by the forks of the Enoree.

By being available for the opportunity that came her way, despite the risk she had to take, Emily Geiger was able to make an important contribution to the cause of independence.

Questions

1. How did Emily demonstrate availability to the cause of freedom?
2. What hardships did she have to undergo to accomplish her mission?
3. What creativity did she show in disposing of the written message?
4. What did her availability and willingness do for the American cause?
5. Think of a job you know needs to be done. How might you benefit your family, church, or friends by making yourself available to help?

Courage

DEFINITION

Standing alone for righteousness and yielding my fears to God

MEMORY VERSE

Be of good courage, and he shall
strengthen your heart,
all ye that hope in the LORD.
Psalm 31:24

Last Stand

Jordan Freeman

Battle of Groton Heights, Connecticut
September 6, 1781

As the town, wharves, and ships exploded in flames, American soldiers fled through the swamps surrounding the harbor at New London, Connecticut. One hundred eighty-five Continental soldiers in homespun clothes, barefoot free Black troops, and their officers in tattered buff-and-blue uniforms fled through the tangled brush beneath a blazing riot of orange and yellow leaves that heralded the New England autumn. Behind them came seventeen hundred British raiders led by Benedict

British landing at Fort Griswold

Arnold. Arnold hoped to break the back of the southern campaign by luring George Washington's army north and away from Lord Cornwallis' troops by launching an attack on the New England port near the Thames River. Jordan Freeman, a forty-nine-year-old Black soldier, measured the distance between the enemy and Fort Griswold perched on the strategic Groton Heights. Reaching the defenses, the men tumbled into the fort and barricaded it behind them.

Both officers and men realized that the British forces outnumbered them hopelessly. Forty-three-year-old Colonel William Ledyard, grimly looking over the handful of ammunition, several small cannons, bayonets, rifles, and pikes, knew that they could not hope to hold out for long. Even so, the American soldiers prepared to make a last stand at all costs. Jordan Freeman crouched near the fort wall, his pike held ready for use. Glancing around, he could see his commander, Colonel Ledyard, sword in hand. Once the colonel's slave, Jordan marveled at how their relationship had metamorphosed, like a chrysalis bursting free of its cocoon, to become a delicate, beautiful winged thing. One day, he was his master's servant, laying out his clean white shirts, arranging his hair, helping him shave. Then, one day, his master came to him, looked him in the eye, and told him that he was free. During the years that followed, their relationship changed and deepened, becoming one of mutual friendship. When the colonel left to command the defense of the town against the British, Jordan Freeman gladly joined, eager to serve under his former master, friend, and commander. As the passing winters slowly grayed his head, the man who gloried in his new name, "freeman," proved that he would do anything to fight for this new republic, and for Lilly, his wife of sixteen years, and for his friend Colonel Ledyard.

Outside Fort Griswold, Benedict Arnold, infuriated by the stubborn American resistance, hurled his seventeen hundred British redcoats at the wall. After the devastation at the town's defenses, Colonel Ledyard commanded only about eighty men. The defenders, running out of ammunition, fought back desperately. From below, the British began yelling for them to surrender, threatening to give no quarter. Hearing this, Colonel Ledyard ordered his men to stop fighting. But a small number struck back as a mass of British soldiers, armed with bayonets, swarmed over the wall.

Suddenly, Major William Montgomery stepped over the wall and demanded to know who commanded the fort.

Colonel William Ledyard faced him. "I did once," he said quietly. "You do now."

He unbuckled his sword and handed it over. Instead of accepting it, the British major seized the sword, twisted it, and thrust it into Colonel Ledyard's body, piercing his white linen shirt and waistcoat. The murdered American officer collapsed on the ground. Jordan Freeman, watching in horror, saw his beloved commander collapse. Without thinking, he raised his bayonet and drove it through the major's crimson uniform.

Seeing their leader fall, the British poured over the wall. Stabbing with their bayonets, they began brutally slaughtering the American soldiers who fought back with empty rifles, bayonets, and pikes. Near the wall, another Black soldier named Lambert bent to pick up the American flag where it lay on the ground beside its splintered pole. He boldly stretched it high over his head, waving it until British soldiers leading the bayonet charge

Jordan Freeman (bottom right) after avenging Colonel Ledyard

surrounded him. Jordan Freeman fell dead only a few minutes after avenging Colonel Ledyard's death. Later, witnesses discovered that he had received thirty-three bayonet wounds during the charge. On that September day near the end of the war, eighty men, black and white, had joined hands against a superior enemy in a last courageous stand. The battle had lasted only forty minutes.

Despite the British victory at Fort Griswold, Benedict Arnold and his redcoats had experienced humiliatingly heavy losses while fighting against only a handful of American troops. Today, on the site where he fell, stands a plaque at Griswold Fort depicting Jordan Freeman stretching up with his spear to kill Major Montgomery. Jordan Freeman, whose name celebrated his life as a freed slave, demonstrated unusual courage both during the

Plaque commemorating Jordan Freeman's courage

battle and by his determination to avenge the murder of Colonel Ledyard, the man who had been both commander and his friend.

The name of Jordan Freeman stands away down, last on the list of heroes – perhaps the greatest hero of them all!

—Parker Pillsbury,
abolitionist, writing to
William Cooper Nell

Questions

1. What type of relationship did Jordan Freeman have with his former owner, Colonel Ledyard?
2. How did Jordan Freeman display courage in defending his country?
3. Tell how he courageously avenged his Colonel's death.
4. How did Colonel Ledyard's men act upon their courage despite being outmanned and having little ammunition?
5. What situations do you face in your life where you could benefit by demonstrating courage?
6. Can you think of a specific situation about which you need to pray to ask God to give you courage?

Generosity

DEFINITION

Giving unselfishly to the needs of others

MEMORY VERSE

Every man according as he purposeth
in his heart, so let him give;
not grudgingly, or of necessity:
for God loveth a cheerful giver.

II Corinthians 9:7

The Generous Man Who Helped America

Haym Solomon

New York City & Philadelphia,
Pennsylvania
October, 1781

The fire broke out mysteriously, starting in a straw-filled stable, along a street somewhere on Manhattan Island. Within minutes, red flames sprang up, licking at walls, burning a deep, midnight blue under creaking wooden stairs, throwing a sulfurous yellow light against the autumn darkness of a New York City night. Just six days earlier, on September 15, the city had fallen to Lord Charles Cornwallis' British army. Fanned by the wind, the hungry flames consumed a quarter of the city, turning four hundred ninety-three houses, in which the occupying British forces planned to quarter troops, into stark black skeletons and swirling ashes.

Haym Solomon

From a distance, a man with dark hair swept into a queue, and a handsome, high-browed face, watched as the city burned. Thirty-six-year-old Haym Solomon could not have wanted this to happen to his beloved adopted city, but he must have known that he might be blamed since he was known to be a member of the New York branch of the Sons of Liberty.

Lord Cornwallis, furious at the destruction of the city, immediately began rounding up suspects from among the Sons of Liberty. As Hessian soldiers (German troops fighting for the British side) began plundering the burned city, Haym Solomon did not have time to escape. Perhaps he did not have time to say goodbye to his young wife, Rachel, and their small child. Hurried from his successful brokerage company in New York City, Solomon found himself charged with helping to set the fire. Condemned without a trial, the young broker was imprisoned in an ancient warehouse called the "Old Sugar House."

Freezing blasts of wind rattled the building, not touching the filth thickening on the floor, but turning the prisoners' faces and bodies blue. There was no fire. Haym Solomon, huddled on the floor of the old warehouse, soon developed a severe cold that settled in his chest. Coughing and gasping for breath in the cold air, he lay crowded among the other prisoners. Pain pressed like a lead weight on his chest. Seeing his weakness and emaciation, the British soldiers moved the young man not to a hospital for treatment, but to "The Provost," a maximum security prison. Under the brutal treatment and neglect, his condition grew steadily worse, settling in his lungs. In this cell, he remembered Poland, the spreading green and yellow croplands of the Polish Corridor. After Russia, Austria, and Prussia divided Poland in 1775, Solomon had fled to Western Europe. During the next few years, he travelled between Europe and New York, polishing his skills in finance and foreign languages. When he first arrived in America, the young financier landed right in the middle of the political turmoil over the issue of resistance to tyranny. Solomon soon put his talents to use, setting up a successful brokerage company in New York City. There, he also met and married Rachel Franks.

Despite his illness, Solomon watched his guards as they changed positions and took turns at guard duty. He recognized their tarred pigtails and high, Hessian peaked helmets. He could understand their thick German accents. He also noticed that the British officers had difficulty communicating with the guards, since the men did not speak English and the British did not speak German. One day, Solomon quietly let it drop that he could speak German. Not wanting to be viewed as a British sympathizer, he made no move to volunteer as an interpreter. Once the British authorities at "The Provost" realized that their frail prisoner could help them, they rushed to move him to better, warmer quarters where he could begin his new job. With his health improved due to a clean room, good food, and better treatment, Solomon began working as a patriot even inside the British prison. Before his release from prison, Solomon had found himself drawn to the center of the American espionage ring as one of the Sons of Liberty. They often met in strange places such as rooms above coffeehouses,

Haym Solomon raising funds to finance the Revolutionary War

the attic of a bookstore, or a lonely road at night. No one outside of the ring knew what they did. Having used his real brokerage business as a cover for his spying activities, Solomon now used his knowledge of the German language to lure more

Monument to Robert Morris, George Washington, and Haym Solomon, Chicago, Illinois

than five hundred Hessian soldiers away from the British to the American side. Finally, the redcoats released their imprisoned interpreter without realizing that he had been inciting their foreign mercenaries to desert.

Two years later, Solomon's dangerous activities brought him face to face with the British authorities once more. Handcuffed and hustled to a gloomy prison called "Congress Hill," Solomon stood before his captors on August 11, 1778, and listened as a drum-head court martial convicted him of capital crimes and condemned him to death. They had already confiscated all his property that he had worked so hard for, his brokerage company, and every penny he owned. Alone in his cell again, the generous broker did not sit and wait for his execution day to arrive. Before his arrest, Solomon had anticipated that he would have trouble getting out of this desperate situation. Planning brilliantly, he concealed his last gold coins in his clothes so skillfully that the British soldiers did not find them. Now, he quietly called a sympathetic or merely greedy guard to his cell, slipped the gold coins into his hand, and disappeared through the open door. Within minutes, he began his secret journey to a new life in Philadelphia, Pennsylvania, sending for Rachel to join him.

In Philadelphia, Solomon began to build up his broker business again from scratch. Setting up his office in a busy coffeehouse in downtown Philadelphia, Solomon worked tirelessly as paymaster for the French army and naval forces in America, as well as negotiator with the Spanish, French, and Dutch ambassadors.

When Congress appointed Robert Morris as Superintendent of Finance in 1781, he asked Solomon to work with him. The diligent broker turned all his energies to negotiating for most of the war aid sent to America from France and Holland. As paymaster for the French foreign military, he sold bills of exchange to colonial merchants to raise funds. More often than not, he reached again and again into his own pocket to support Continental Congress Delegates James Madison and James Wilson when they travelled to Philadelphia. Madison confessed: "I have for some time . . . been a pensioner on the favor of Haym Solomon, a ... broker."

At a time and in a society that too often harshly viewed all Jews as moneylenders, Haym Solomon consistently gave his own money to the American cause, asking prices far below market interest rates, and never asking to be paid back. He often helped men who gained little or no recognition for the role that they played during the revolution. Learning that Dr. Bodo Otto, a sixty-five-year-old surgeon in the Continental Army, had founded the hospital at Valley Forge and spent the last cent he owned to buy medical supplies, Solomon granted Otto a monetary bequest without asking for repayment. Due to Solomon's gift, the doctor found himself able to reestablish his own medical practice in Reading,

Pennsylvania, at the end of the war.

In August 1781, General Washington, aided by the Count de Rochambeau, encircled Lord Cornwallis at Yorktown, Virginia. As his men sat in the trenches, Washington knew that he needed at least $20,000 to press on with his campaign and force Cornwallis to surrender. But he had no funds. Writing to Robert Morris, Washington begged him to raise money to finance this campaign. He also turned to his aide and said, "Send for Haym Solomon," another man he could trust to help get the job done. Solomon and Morris flew into action, raising the badly-needed $20,000 through the sale of bills of exchange so that Washington could push his Yorktown campaign to final victory at the Treaty of Paris.

Haym Solomon only outlived the Revolution by four years. Suffering from tuberculosis contracted during his harsh imprisonments, he died at age forty-four, leaving Rachel and four small children in poverty. Later, his family appealed to Congress to repay the debt, but the Government of the Confederation had no power to levy or collect taxes. Swamped with debts to foreign allies and focused on issuing pensions to disabled veterans, Congress rejected the Solomon's requests for repayment.

Today, a monument featuring Haym Solomon, George Washington, and Robert Morris stands on

East Wacker Drive in Chicago, Illinois. A portion of the inscription on the plaque reads: "The government of the United States which gives to bigotry no sanction, to the persecution no assistance, requires only that they who live under its protection should demean [conduct] themselves as good citizens in giving it on all occasions their effectual support." President George Washington 1790.

Haym Solomon demonstrated generosity, in the words of a commemorative stamp, by "raising most of the money needed to finance the American Revolution and later to save the new nation from collapse."

Questions

1. Why was Haym Solomon suspected of starting a fire on Manhattan Island? Was he falsely accused?
2. What was his punishment? Describe his hardships during his imprisonment.
3. What act on Solomon's part helped earn him better treatment?
4. How did his knowledge of the German language benefit him again?
5. Why was Solomon slated to be hanged?
6. How did he escape his sentence?
7. How did he start life anew once he escaped?
8. What quality did Haym Solomon demonstrate that greatly benefited the American cause?
9. Tell of his generosity to the 65-year-old surgeon.
10. What caused Washington to depend upon Haym Solomon?
11. Who in your sphere of influence could benefit greatly from your generosity? brother? sister? parents? neighbors? widows? church members?

Thoroughness

DEFINITION

Bringing to completion each task I do with excellence

MEMORY VERSE

Better is the end of a thing than the beginning thereof: and the patient in spirit is better than the proud in spirit.

Ecclesiastes 7:8

We the People

James Madison

Montpelier, Virginia & Philadelphia,
Pennsylvania
May–July, 1787

The dull grey winter day pressed against the windows at Montpelier, clouding the natural light and making it difficult for him to read his scribbled notes. When he rose from his desk, James Madison stood five feet, four inches tall in his black buckled shoes. As he worked into the night, he searched through his notes for his amended copy of George Mason's draft of the *Virginia Declaration of Rights.* Dated June 8, 1776, this document had been the first step toward independence and the drafting of a Constitution. Madison's new draft reminded him

James Madison

of the long hours sweating through the Virginia Resolutions that year and later as a delegate to the Continental Congress.

Four years before, the Revolutionary War ended with the Treaty of Paris, sealing America as a nation independent of Great Britain. But the colonies now faced a different issue. Until now, the autonomous colonies had been held together by the Articles of Confederation, a military alliance designed to help fight the War for Independence. But the Articles of Confederation lacked strength. A government founded on these articles had no power to tax. It also could not pay its outstanding debts from the Revolutionary War period. Prominent members of the Continental Congress, including George Washington, feared that the union would break up and dissolve into bankruptcy. To this end, delegates from twelve of the thirteen colonies agreed to meet in Philadelphia in order to redefine the social compact between the states, the national government, and the people.

The delegates for the Constitutional Convention began arriving in Philadelphia on May 25, 1787. Many of them had participated in drafting the Declaration of Independence and the Articles of Confederation. Now they had to discuss revising the Articles of Confederation. They crowded into the brick hall, filling the wooden Windsor chairs in front of the tall, light windows. Immediately they elected George Washington president of the Convention. Then they sat down to work. But the task proved more difficult than they had anticipated. Those that favored a strong central government argued against those who feared that a national government would trample on the rights of the states. Many worried that the autonomy enjoyed by the diverse Northern, Middle and Southern colonies during the Revolution would make them unwilling to accept a new authority.

Finally, after five days of hot debate, they scrapped the weak Articles of Confederation and began on a new body of law for government. They believed that "a national government ought to be established consisting of a supreme Legislative, Executive and Judiciary."

A linguist and political theorist with a brilliant mind, James Madison came to the forefront in the proposed draft for a new constitution. As an ultranationalist (those extremely devoted to the interests of the burgeoning nation), Madison also led the faction arguing for a strong central government. In the months preceding the Convention, Madison had framed an outline, "Vices of the Political System of the US," attacking the Articles of Confederation. The delegates now used Madison's outline as a basis for the "Virginia Plan of Government." These nationalists opened the debate with a call to favor the large states, like Virginia, and give great power to the new federal government. The argument continued through May and into the summer as delegates disputed and compromised.

Meanwhile, James Madison worked determinedly on framing the language and political structure of the new document. The small delegate from Virginia rose often to argue or explain. Over the next four months, he spoke more than two hundred times. His fellow members listened in admiration as he debated Patrick Henry's view that sovereignty should rest with the state legislatures. Despite his powerful and persuasive words, Madison sometimes lost his battles. At the same time, he weaned delegates' minds away from the idea of the autonomous state and instead toward the notion of a federal government. From 1619 until now, the thirteen colonies had operated somewhat independently with their own legislatures and Houses of Assembly controlled by royal governors. The idea of a large federal government ruling the states did not appeal to those who feared that it would infringe on the rights of the people.

During these debates, Madison worked fiercely and quietly. He scribbled notes during the hot debates, refusing to let anyone read them. He pushed

Signing of the United States Constitution, September 17, 1787

for a balance of power between the states and the federal government. While Gouverneur Morris headed the committee after the delegates had finished their resolutions, James Madison did most of the writing. The founders had a strong belief that the Bible holds the answers to men's problems and is the blueprint for life. They relied heavily on a book by John Locke called *The Two Treatises of Government*. This book, although only about four hundred pages long, refers to the Bible fifteen hundred times! Political scientists from Texas completed a ten-year study in which they analyzed the writing of the founders to see where they got their specific ideas. As they examined the sources, they found the Bible was quoted far more than any other source. Thirty-four percent of the quotes were from the Bible!

Madison also adapted portions from the Articles of Confederation and inserted and rewrote parts of other states' constitutions to create a strong, sublime, and unified whole. In his view, the three branches, legislative, executive, and judiciary, played against each other, together creating a balance of power that ensured that none of the three branches would grow stronger than the others.

The delegates also came to an agreement about representation in Congress with the Great Compromise. This compromise combined elements of the Virginia Plan, which urged representation based on population, with the New Jersey Plan, which argued for equal representation. To this end, the members worked out the Three-Fifths Compromise: a balance of power that counted every five slaves as three people for representation purposes. If Virginia counted all of its white and slave population for representation, it would tip the balance of power in Congress heavily in favor of the slave states. If they did not count slaves at all, then the balance of power would tip towards the northern colonies. The members concluded that an equal balance of representation worked out to a three-fifths compromise. The purpose of the three-fifths rule was not to devalue slaves, but to weaken the slave states' power.

The members met on eighty-nine of the one hundred sixteen days between May 25th and the middle of September. Always tiny and frail, Madison's weight dropped to one hundred pounds due to the stress. As the day appointed for the Convention approached, Madison still feared failure. Worried, he confessed in a letter to his lifelong friend Thomas Jefferson, then acting as minister to France, that the plan would not work on the federal level or that rebellion would break out in those areas opposed to a strong central government. He understood the crisis clearly: "Thirteen sovereignties pulling against each other, and all tugging at the federal head, will soon bring ruin on the whole."

September 17th dawned at Independence Hall. Twelve of the thirteen states had sent delegates, with the exception of Rhode Island, which feared that a strong central government would prove disadvantageous to the smaller states. As James Madison watched and listened with anxiety, thirty-nine of the forty-two delegates present voted to approve the Constitution. Madison's words would echo through history: "We the People of the United States, in Order to form a more perfect Union, establish Justice, insure domestic Tranquility, provide for the common defense, promote the general Welfare, and secure the Blessings of Liberty to ourselves and our Posterity, do ordain and establish this Constitution for the United States of America."

The road to the Constitution had been a long one, and many of the founders worked together to make it a reality. The document still had to go to the Congress of the Confederation. From there, the Congress distributed it to the states for ratification. If nine states ratified it, then the new constitution would become law. Delaware stepped in to ratify the Constitution, then New Hampshire, nine months later. At last, on May 29, 1790, the final state, Rhode Island, ratified the Constitution.

The anti-federalists, however, refused to accept the Constitution if it did not contain a Bill of Rights. The federalists answered these concerns by printing their arguments in serial newspapers and pamphlets that became known as the "Federalist Papers." Although Madison believed that the Constitution already protected human rights, he realized the need for people to know that their individual rights would be guaranteed and protected by the federal government. In response, he worked to merge the two opposing groups into a solid base that approved and supported the Constitution. He pushed the Bill of Rights through Congress, allowing the Constitution to go into effect as law in 1789.

Madison's thoroughness in helping give birth to the Constitution would earn him the nickname "Father of the Constitution."

The real wonder is that so many difficulties should have been surmounted with a unanimity almost as unprecedented as it must have been expected . . . It is impossible for the man of pious reflection not to perceive in it a finger of that Almighty hand which has been so frequently and signally extended to our relief in the critical stages of the revolution.

—*James Madison*

Questions

1. What was James Madison working on so intently?
2. Why were the Articles of Confederation no longer adequate?
3. What did the Constitutional Congress and George Washington fear?
4. Who was elected president of the Convention?
5. What was the main difference to be reconciled?
6. Who proposed drafting a new constitution?
7. What document was the Constitution based upon?
8. What was Madison's greatest concern if the plan did not work?
9. What did the anti-federalists insist on before voting for the Constitution? Why?
10. What nickname was given to James Madison?
11. How did thoroughness aid in researching for and writing such a crucial document?

Prudence

DEFINITION

Exercising caution in all situations; foreseeing the consequences of my actions

MEMORY VERSE

A prudent man foreseeth the trouble and hides himself: but the simple pass on and are punished.

Proverbs 22:3

Rising Sun

Benjamin Franklin

Philadelphia
June 28, 1787

They arrived secretly, rolling in carriages up to the door of the Pennsylvania State House. Inside, they flashed signed credentials to the guards standing ramrod-straight beside the door to the council chamber. Not a single rumor of what was about to take place must leak to the outside world. Creaking across the wooden floors, the men slid into their places at long tables covered with green baize, flanked by tall windows that let in the natural light. No one could talk, page through documents,

Independence Hall Council Chamber

read books or flip through papers while someone spoke. The delegates all shifted and looked towards the dais as the President of the Constitutional Convention, George Washington, rose to open the meeting.

The convention's leaders made some hard, fast rules. Each state would only be allowed one vote. The majority of the delegation from that state must be present at the convention and express agreement in order for their vote to be counted. Each man could only speak twice on each issue before everyone else had their turn. Polls were taken often to test the delegates' mood. When a speaker rose, he had to face the convention President at the head of the room. He could not turn to any of the other delegates, address angry words to a specific individual or engage in direct confrontation.

Arriving with the others before May 28th, Virginia delegate James Madison felt that the Articles of Confederation, with their weak authority, inability to tax, and decentralized structure, should be abandoned and a new plan drawn up. The smaller states, particularly New Jersey, objected. They favored simply making amendments to the Articles of Confederation. After heated debate, it became clear that nothing could fix the fundamentally flawed Articles of Confederation. Once they agreed to scrap the Articles, the delegates rushed to write up a new system. Virginia came up with the "Fifteen Resolves," which came to form the basis of the Convention's agenda. A month passed in furious debate as the list grew to twenty-three "Resolves." By June, they hung deadlocked on three major issues: slavery, regulation of commerce, and how representation should be determined for each state. Out of forty-one Virginia proposals, twelve were rejected, accompanied by two near rejections. It soon became clear that the delegates had not come to fix their rubber stamp to a document and then go home.

Feeling threatened by Virginia, the small states counterattacked. On June 14, New Jersey delegate William Patterson asked for the day off to draw up a new plan for the smaller states. He intended to present it next day. On June 15th, Patterson announced the New Jersey Plan. Favoring the smaller, and mostly northern, states, the New Jersey Plan offered scarcely anything new in the form of government. Instead, it called for a broad, unicameral legislature and a president who would be elected, like a king, for life. The smaller states had in fact merely reworked portions of the Articles of Confederation and presented it back to the Convention.

Just then, Alexander Hamilton, delegate from New York, rose. It is too dangerous to walk on untried waters, he argued. We ought to go back to the safe British government system. Heads nodded across the room, but no one moved to support his idea. Since none of the delegates seriously considered adopting a British form of government, with a monarch, Parliament and a House of Lords, they did not bother to vote on Hamilton's motion.

Small and slight, James Madison rose to his feet. His voice filled with emotion, Madison declared that they should draw up a "Constitution for the Ages." Only the Virginia Plan, he believed, would stand the test of time. The delegates voted down the New Jersey Plan on the spot. But the decision on June 19 only sparked further argument. Moving onto more heated and delicate questions, the debates soon turned into quarreling. As the summer sun blazed down on the Philadelphia streets outside, the debates escalated to a crisis point.

Then on June 28th, eighty-one-year-old Benjamin Franklin could stand it no longer. He rose to his feet, his grey hair slipping onto his shoulders. All around him, men bickered and argued, locked in bitter debate. Franklin turned towards George Washington, who listened with a look of despair on his dignified face. As president, he had sat silently through the long, heated arguments, only intervening to call the meeting to order.

Benjamin Franklin

"Mr. President . . ." Franklin's voice cut through the angry hubbub.

"In the beginning of the Contest with Great Britain, when we were sensible of danger, we had daily prayer in this room for Divine protection. Our prayers, Sir, were heard, and they were graciously answered. All of us who were engaged in the struggle must have observed frequent instances of a superintending Providence in our favor.

"To that kind Providence we owe this happy opportunity of consulting in peace on the means of establishing our future national felicity. And have we now forgotten that powerful Friend? Or do we imagine we no longer need His assistance?"

Franklin expressed his hope that when the delegates next assembled it would be with a determination to draft a new constitution. If they could not agree on everything individually, then at least they ought to draft a constitution that would be the best under the circumstances.

Washington's face brightened. A ray of light seemed to have entered the room with Franklin's words.

"I have lived, Sir, a long time, and the longer I live, the more convincing proofs I see of this truth—that God governs in the affairs of men. And if a sparrow cannot fall to the ground without His notice, is it probable that an empire can rise without His aid?

"We have been assured, Sir, in the Sacred Writings, that 'except the Lord build the House, they labor in vain that build it.' I firmly believe this; and I also believe that without His concurring aid we shall succeed in this political building no better than the builders of Babel: We shall be divided by our partial local interests; our projects will be confounded, and we ourselves shall become a reproach and bye word down to future ages. And what is worse, mankind may hereafter this unfortunate instance, despair of establishing Governments by Human Wisdom, and leave it to chance, war, and conquest."

Franklin continued with weight and authority.

The Rising Sun Chair

"I will suggest, Mr. President, that propriety of nominating and appointing . . . a chaplain to this Convention, whose duty it shall be uniformly to assemble with us, and introduce the business of each day by an address to the Creator of the universe, and the Governor of all nations, beseeching Him to preside in our council, enlighten our minds with a portion of heavenly wisdom, influence our hearts with a love of truth and justice, and crown our labors with complete and abundant success!"

As Franklin sat down, a smile broke out over George Washington's dignified face as he sat in the president's chair. Roger Sherman seconded the motion. Admiring silence greeted Franklin's speech. Faces calmed. A number of delegates felt as if they had witnessed an historic speech on the floor of the Roman Senate. Franklin's prudent words diffused the growing tension, creating a sobering effect. When the delegates again pulled up to the tables, they worked harder than before. But now, while disagreements still surfaced, the men determined to work out their differences with the view to creating a better, more stable United States of America.

Although Franklin suggested that the Convention call in a minister to offer daily prayers as a chaplain and Roger Sherman seconded it, the motion did not pass. Hamilton and a number of other delegates pointed out that professional ministers insisted on payment for making prayers, but the Convention did not have any money to pay them.

As the delegates tidied up their work on September 17th, having adopted James Madison's new Constitution, Benjamin Franklin looked towards the president's chair on the dais. A painted sun, golden and rising, shone on the back of it. Franklin pointed it out, seizing the attention of everyone in the room.

"I have," he said thoughtfully, "often in the course of the Session, and the vicissitudes of my hopes and fears as to its issue, looked at that behind the President without being able to tell whether it was rising or setting." He paused, full of the hope, pride and freedom that the new Constitution offered. "But now at length I have the happiness to know that it is a rising and not a setting Sun."

Benjamin Franklin demonstrated prudence with his careful speech, calming the minds of the Founding Fathers and redirecting their priorities. By pointing the delegates to God who had helped them win the American Revolution, Franklin also gave them hope that they could settle their disagreements and create a new Constitution.

I have lived, Sir, a long time, and the longer I live, the more convincing proofs I see of this truth—that God governs in the affairs of men. And if a sparrow cannot fall to the ground without His notice, is it probable that an empire can rise without His aid?

—Benjamin Franklin

Questions

1. What were the delegates assembling to decide upon?
2. Why were the "Fifteen Resolves" met with such controversy?
3. What did the New Jersey plan favor?
4. What did Alexander Hamilton suggest?
5. What was James Madison's solution?
6. What did Benjamin Franklin finally rise to his feet and suggest implementing?
7. How did Franklin's words affect the assembly?
8. Read again Franklin's famous words on pages 101-103?. What did Franklin propose?
9. Who seconded his motion?
10. What was Franklin's thought as he observed the rising sun carved on the President's chair?
11. How did Franklin demonstrate prudence in settling the dispute and setting direction?
12. How can you use discretion by foreseeing consequences of your actions before carrying them out?
13. Think of an instance of a person in Scripture who demonstrated prudence.

Uprightness

DEFINITION

Adhering strictly to moral principles; righteous

MEMORY VERSE

He that walketh in his uprightness feareth the LORD: but he that is perverse in his ways despiseth him.

Proverbs 14:2

Searching Out the Best

Thomas Jefferson

Washington, D.C.
Winter, 1804

On a cold winter evening in 1804, the red-haired third President of the United States sat with penknife in hand, poring over two copies of the Bible. From each of the red Moroccan leather volumes he cut into the woven paper and carefully excised the words of Jesus. He then pasted the fragments onto the blank pages of a folio book. Two nights later, Jefferson completed the work and in the typically wordy style of the day titled it, "The Philosophy of Jesus of Nazareth, being Extracted

One of the Bibles from which Jefferson extracted the words of Jesus

from the Account of His Life and Doctrines given by Matthew, Mark, Luke, and John; Being an Abridgement of the New Testament for the Use of the Indians, Unembarrassed with Matters of Fact or Faith Beyond the Level of their Comprehensions."

Jefferson finished his project a night or two later but history has denied us the privilege of seeing his work because no original copy of it is with us today. Still, his long title tells us his intention. He was creating a collection of the teachings of Jesus from Scripture for the use of the Native American tribes. Jefferson knew, as did nearly everyone else in his day, that the doctrines of Jesus are life-changing and stand forever as the purest teachings on virtuous living ever written.

Jefferson's investment of two evenings in such a work, despite the many pressures of his office, would come as no surprise to those who knew him then or those who have studied his life in the two centuries since. Thomas Jefferson's respect for Christ and the Bible were well-known. Modern secularists have tried to paint him as an atheist or agnostic, cherry-picking quotes from his many writings, but the fact is that Jefferson made a lifelong study of the famous moral teachers of all time and found the words of Jesus to be vastly superior to any other.

His reverence for the Bible is obvious from his own record books, which show that on numerous occasions he contributed from his own funds toward the printing of Bibles. He also was passionately interested in sending the Bible message to the Native American tribes. One historian wrote of:

> "... Jefferson's interest in Christian missions to the Native Americans in a way that many modern scholars have dismissed as irrelevant. This dismissal has led to the misunderstand ing of Jefferson's motives for his compilation of Christ's teachings. Jefferson had a deep, genuine commitment to missionary efforts among the Indians. His account books show

that he consistently donated his own money to missionaries and to societies that distributed Bibles to both Americans and Indians."

Jefferson also believed that America would be a better place if the government made an investment in this work. In 1803, President Jefferson signed a treaty with the Kaskaskia Indians to provide them with ministerial care and the construction of a church building. The next year, he signed into law another federal act for "propagating the Gospel" among the numerous tribes.

While President, Jefferson was in faithful attendance at the church services held in the Capitol building each Sunday. Even bad weather would not keep him away. He said to a friend, "No nation has ever existed or been governed without religion—nor can be. The Christian religion is the best religion that has been given to man and I, as Chief Magistrate of this nation, am bound to give it the sanction of my example." During his years as President, worship services were also established in the federally-owned buildings housing the national Treasury and the War Department.

Jefferson believed the Bible to be of great benefit to those who would read it and apply its teachings to their lives. So his short book with the long title was just another of his efforts to bring that to pass.

In modern times, critics have referred to this book or a later one, compiled in 1820 as "Jefferson's

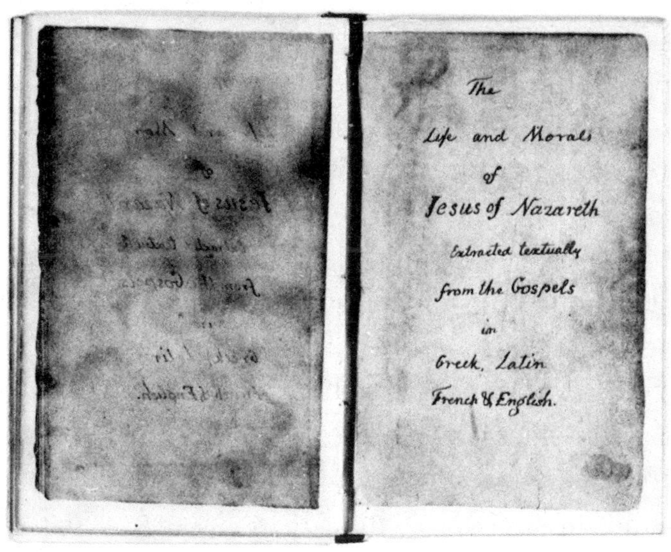

Title Page from "The Life and Morals of Jesus of Nazareth"

Bible" and claimed that he had removed all references to the supernatural happenings given in the Gospels. But a reconstruction of the book based on his own handwritten list of the passages he included, plus the two actual Bibles he used (revealing the passages he clipped out and pasted in his book), shows that he included the healing on the Sabbath from Luke 14:1–6, the Lord's commission to His disciples to go and heal the sick and raise the dead from Matthew 10, and His teaching about His own resurrection from the dead. In addition, there are His second coming, His role as Judge of men, and His place as Son of God and Lord of a heavenly kingdom. There are many other references to His supernatural nature and power, which the critics conveniently forget to mention—if they are even honest enough to do real research into Jefferson's Native American book.

Jefferson wrote to a friend that he regretted having so little time to dedicate to this book because of the weight of the workload he bore as President. He expressed the hope that he would one day be able to do a similar condensation of the Gospels with better preparation and more time to invest. He finally found the time to begin in 1813 and completed the project in 1820.

This second book is also sometimes mistakenly called the "Jefferson Bible," but that is obviously not what he intended. He titled it *The Life and Morals of Jesus of Nazareth,* and he made it plain on numerous occasions that its purpose was to collect and present the major moral teachings of Jesus in one short and simple volume. It was not intended to be a Bible or a condensation of the entire New Testament.

Jefferson had for decades been a devoted student of virtue, or the discipline of ethics. He had read the moral teachings of the most famous philosophers of all times and compared them with each other and with the Bible. He found the words of Jesus far superior to any other, and for that reason wanted a book of His own teachings to read and meditate upon with no comments from others—even the Apostles. When finished, the book contained "forty-six pages of pure and unsophisticated doctrines such as were professed and acted on by the unlettered Apostles, the Apostolic Fathers, and the Christians of the first century," as he wrote to his friend, John Adams.

Well then, if Jefferson's first booklet was written for the Native Americans, who was the second work intended for? The answer to this question can be

President Thomas Jefferson

found in the words of Thomas Jefferson Randolph, Jefferson's eldest grandson. He wrote that his grandfather had "left two codifications of the morals of Jesus—one for himself, and another for the Indians; the first of which I now possess . . . His codification of *The Morals of Jesus* was not known to his family before his death, and they learnt from a letter addressed to a friend that he was in the habit of reading nightly from it before going to bed." Obviously, Jefferson produced *The Morals of Jesus* for his own study and benefit.

In 1886, Cyrus Adler, the librarian of the Smithsonian, located the original copy that had belonged to Jefferson's grandson and arranged for Congress to purchase it. In 1900, representative of Iowa, Congressman John Lacy, impressed by Jefferson's compilation, sponsored a congressional resolution that Congress reprint Jefferson's *Morals of Jesus of Nazareth* for use by the nation's senators and congressmen. Congress passed Lacy's resolution and printed nine thousand copies at government expense. For the next fifty years, a copy of *The Life and Morals of Jesus of Nazareth* was given to every senator and congressmen at their swearing in!

The religious beliefs of Thomas Jefferson are still being debated by scholars and will be for a long time to come. Those who wish to paint him as an immoral, irreligious man have produced many lies about him. As far as we know, Jefferson never received salvation through faith in Christ. Throughout his life he diligently studied and debated many aspects of religion and virtue. He was determined to leave no stone unturned in his search for true moral principles. But what is clear about Thomas Jefferson is that, after decades of reading the works of men regarded as the great moral teachers of all time, he was forced to conclude that the real truth was to be found in the words of Jesus, and daily perusing those very words, he strove to become a man of uprightness!

Questions

1. What words did Jefferson cut from the Bible?
2. What did he then do with the words extracted from the Bible?
3. Why did he choose the words of Jesus to spread among the Native Americans tribes?
4. What did he entitle this document?
5. What actions did Thomas Jefferson take during his lifetime that proved he had a deep respect for the Bible?
6. What did he say concerning the Christian religion?
7. Thomas Jefferson a second time undertook the task of extracting the words of Jesus from a Bible. For what purpose did he do this and how did he make use of this document? What did he entitle it?
8. Why did he purpose to meditate on the words of Jesus?
9. When did Congress reprint this manuscript? For what purpose?
10. What quality did Jefferson strive to pursue in his personal life aided by the use of this document?

11. Revisionist history has given us a faulty view of Mr. Jefferson. They wish us to believe (and many good Christians have unknowingly believed the lie) that Jefferson cut out the words of Jesus because he chose not to obey them. It is your job to arm yourself with the truth and learn to articulate it to others. Be prepared to share this truth with others.

Discernment

DEFINITION

The ability to identify
subtle untruths or motives

MEMORY VERSE

But the LORD said unto Samuel, Look not on his countenance, or on the height of his stature; because I have refused him: for the LORD seeth not as man seeth; for man looketh on the outward appearance, but the LORD looketh on the heart.

I Samuel 16:7

The Secret of America

Alexis de Tocqueville

May 9, 1831–February 20, 1832

The young man wore his dark hair full and curly in the style of King Louis-Philippe, Tsar Alexander I, and several heads of the Holy Alliance who dominated European politics during the first quarter of the 19th century. His French accent slightly curled up the end of his words, making even his statements sound like questions. Twenty-six-year-old Alexis de Tocqueville, descendant of an old Norman aristocratic family, found himself asking countless questions as he opened creaking wooden doors and entered the brick cells of America's prison system.

Sent to America by Louis-Philippe's constitutional July Monarchy (1830–1838), liberal politician Alexis de Tocqueville was a man on a mission. In the context of the nineteenth century, a liberal politician had a much different agenda and worldview than a twentieth-century counterpart. As a liberal speaker, de Tocqueville supported abolition—the freeing of Black slaves. Although de Tocqueville stood for fringe causes in his time, he would also later oppose the concept of socialism during the brief revolution of 1848.

Arriving at Newport, Rhode Island, on May 9, 1831, and pushing west to Green Bay, Michigan, north to Quebec, and as far south as New Orleans, de Tocqueville's bright, intelligent eyes now took in everything. He had come to the United States of America in a quest for practical knowledge and to discover what had made America a success in its struggle against autocracy, when countries like his native France had tried that same experiment and failed.

De Tocqueville weighed the political stability of the United States against what he saw as the increasing political instability of Europe. The Napoleonic wars, which came on the heels of the French revolution, combined with continuing unrest in France and the ascension to the Russian

Alexis de Tocqueville

throne of Tsar Nicholas I, known as the "gendarme (policeman) of Europe," set off a flurry of initially anti-revolutionary alliances that would set the trend for a dangerously allied Europe.

While de Tocqueville toured prisons and discussed such issues as racism, religion, money, the class system, the press, and the role of the government, he also expanded on these topics in his most famous work: his two-volume *Democracy in America.* After studying the American penal system for eighteen months, de Tocqueville sought to understand the essence of American culture and its values. Intrigued by the success of the American dream, the young French philosopher is credited with this quote on America's greatness.

> "I sought for the greatness and genius of America in her commodious harbors and her ample rivers—and it was not there," he observed. ". . . In her fertile fields and boundless forests and it was not there . . .; in her rich mines and her vast world commerce—and it was not there . . .; in her democratic Congress and her matchless Constitution—and it was not there. Not until I went into the churches of America and heard her pulpits flame with righteousness did I understand the secret of her genius and power. America is great because she is good, and if America ever ceases to be good, she will cease to be great."

Alexis de Tocqueville arrived near the start of the American Industrial Revolution, westward expansion, and a new surge in invention. By the time he left the United States in the winter of 1832, the Frenchman had lived there during the ministries of the evangelist Peter Cartwright, revivalist Charles G. Finney, and others. De Tocqueville's discernment in discovering the true secret to America's greatness is inspiring to us today as we realize that our heritage as Americans is truly a godly one!

Nothing is more wonderful than the art of being free, but nothing is harder to learn how to use than freedom.

—Alexis de Tocqueville,
in his book Democracy in America

Questions

1. What conclusion did de Tocqueville reach concerning what made America great?
2. How did this demonstrate discernment?
3. What warning did he give that we should heed today?
4. For what situations should you learn to exercise greater discernment?
5. Think of a situation you've been in where you didn't discern carefully between good and evil and it caused you trouble.

Selected Bibliography

Adams, John, and L. H. Butterfield. *Diary and Autobiography of John Adams, Vol. II.* Cambridge: Harvard University Press, 1962.

Aldridge, Alfred O. *Benjamin Franklin and Nature's God.* Durham, NC: Duke University Press, 1967.

Allison, Robert. *The Boston Massacre.* Beverly, MA: Applewood Books, 2006.

Amler, Jane Frances. *Haym Solomon: Patriot Banker of the American Revolution.* Powerkids Press, 2004.

Ammon, Richard. *Valley Forge.* Holiday House, 2006.

Anderson, Fred. *Crucible of War: The Seven Years' War and the Fate of Empire in British North America: 1754-1766.* New York: Alfred A. Knopf, 2000.

Archer, Richard. *As if an Enemy's Country: the British Occupation of Boston and the Origins of Revolution.* Oxford, New York: Oxford University Press, 2010.

Barton, Charles D. *The Bulletproof George Washington.* Wallbuilders Press, 1990.

Barton, David. *The Jefferson Lies.* Thomas Nelson, 2012 (This is an excellent book and we highly recommend it. It is thoroughly documented and also dispels other myths about Jefferson so prevalently believed today.)

Beliles, Mark A. and Stephen K. McDowell. *America's Providential History.* Charlottesville, VA: Providence Foundation, 1989.

Bessette, Joseph M. and John J. Pitney, Jr. *American Government and Politics: Deliberation, Democracy and Citizenship.* Boston: Wadsworth Cengage Learning, 2011.

Billias, George Athan. *General John Glover and his Marblehead Mariners.* New York: Holt, Rinehart & Winston, 1960.

Bobrick, Benson. *Angel in the Whirlwind: The Triumph of the American Revolution.* New York: Simon & Schuster, 2011.

Bodie, Idella. *The Man Who Loved the Flag.* Heroes and Heroines of the American Revolution. 2008.

Bowdoin, James, Samuel Adams, et al. *A Short Narrative of the Horrid Massacre.* London: W. Bingley, 1770.

Bowen, Catherine Drinker. *Miracle at Philadelphia: The Story of the Constitutional Convention: May to September 1787.* New York: Book-of-the-Month Club, Inc., 1986.

Boyd, Julian P. and Gerard W. Gawalt. *The Declaration of Independence: The Evolution of the Text.* University Press of New England, 1999.

Brady, Patricia. *Martha Washington: An American Life.* New York: Viking Press, 2005.

Brandt, Clare. *The Man in the Mirror: A Life of Benedict Arnold.* New York: Random House, 1994.

Brookhiser, Richard. *James Madison.* Basic Books, 2011.

Brooks, Victor. *The Boston Campaign.* Conshohocken, PA: Combined Publishing, 1999.

Buchanan, John. *The Road to Valley Forge: How Washington Built the Army that Won the Revolution.* Wiley, 2004.

Burnett, Edward Cody. *The Continental Congress.* New York: Norton, 1941.

Burnham, Norman Hammond. *The Battle of Groton Heights: A Story of the Storming of Fort Griswold and the Burning of New London, on the Sixth of September, 1781.* Kessinger Publishing, 2006.

Carbone, Gerald M. *Nathanael Greene: A Biography of the American Revolution.* New York: Palgrave Macmillan, 2010.

Carstens, Kenneth C. and Nancy Son Carstens, eds. *The Life of George Rogers Clark, 1752-1818: Triumphs and Tragedies.* Westport, CT: Praeger, 2004.

Cheney, Lynne. *When Washington Crossed the Delaware: A Wintertime Story for Young Patriots.* New York: Simon & Schuster, 2012.

Chernow, Ron. *Washington: A Life.* New York: Penguin Press, 2010.

Clary, David A. *George Washington's First War: His Early Military Adventures.* New York: Simon & Schuster, 2011.

Coffin, Charles L. *The Boys of '76.* Weiner Media, 2009.

Collier, Christopher. *Decision in Philadelphia: The Constitutional Convention of 1787.* New York: Ballantine Books, 2007.

Collins, Kathleen. *Marquis de Lafayette: French Hero of the American Revolution.* Rosen Central, 2004.

Connecticut Society of the Sons of the American Revolution. *King George's Head.* Sons of the American Revolution, Winter, 1998.

Cooley, Timothy Mather. *Sketches of the Life and Character of the Reverend Samuel Haynes, A.M., for Many Years Pastor of a Church in Rutland, Vermont, and Late in Granville, New York.* New York: Negro Universities Press, 1969.

Copp, John J. *The Battle of Groton Heights: The Massacre of Fort Griswold; and the Burning of New London.* Groton Heights Centennial Committee, 1879.

Crocker, Thomas E. *Braddock's March: How the Man Sent to Seize a Continent Changed American History.* Westholme Publishing, 2011.

Crofut, W. A. and John M. Morris. *The Military and Civil History of Connecticut during the War of 1861-65.* Ledyard Bill, 1868.

Dameron, J. David. *Kings Mountain: The Defeat of the Loyalists, October 7, 1780.* Cambridge, MA: DaCapo Press, 2003.

Davis, Burke. *Black Heroes of the American Revolution.* Sandpiper, 1992.

Dawson, Thomas Fulton. *Life and Character of Edward Oliver Wolcott, Late a Senator of the United States From the State of Colorado.* Forgotten Books, 2012.

Derleth, August. *Vincennes: Portal to the West.* Englewood Cliffs, NJ: Prentice-Hall, 1968.

Dorson, Richard M., *Patriots of the American Revolution: True Accounts by Great Americans from Ethan Allen to George Rogers Clark.* New York: Gramercy Books, 1953.

Driver, Carl S. *John Sevier: Pioneer of the Old Southwest.* Chapel Hill: University of North Carolina Press, 1932.

Dunkerly, Robert M. *The Battle of King's Mountain: Eyewitness Accounts.* The History Press, 2007.

Field, Joseph E. *"Worthy Partner": The Papers of Martha Washington*. Praeger Press, 1994.

Finger, John R. *Tennessee Frontiers: Three Regions in Transition.* Indiana University Press, 2001.

Fischer, David Hackett. *Paul Revere's Ride.* New York: Oxford University Press, 1994.

—. *Washington's Crossing.* Oxford University Press, 2006.

Fleming, Thomas. *Washington's Secret War: The Hidden History of Valley Forge.* Harper Perennial, 2006.

Flexner, James Thomas. *The Traitor and the Spy: Benedict Arnold and John Andre.* New York: Little, Brown & Company, 1975.

Foreman, Samuel A. *Dr. Joseph Warren: The Boston Tea Party, Bunker Hill, and the Birth of American Liberty.* New York: Pelican Publishing, 2011.

Freedman, Russell. *Washington at Valley Forge.* Holiday House: 2008.

Frothingham, Richard. *The Life and Times of Joseph Warren.* Applewood Books, 2009.

Fritz, Jean. *Why Not Lafayette?* New York: Puffin, 2001.

Garrison, Webb. *White House Ladies: Fascinating Tales and Colorful Curiosities.* Tennessee: Thomas Nelson Press, 1996.

Gingrich, Newt. *Valley Forge.* St. Martin's Griffin, 2011.

Golway, Terry. *Washington's General: Nathanael Greene and the Triumph of the American Revolution.* New York: Holt, 2005.

Goodrich, Charles A. *Lives of the Signers to the Declaration of Independence.* New York: Thomas Mather, 1832.

Gordon, William. *The History of the Rise, Progress, and Establishment, of the Independence of the United States of America.* Berkeley: University of California Collection, 1788.

Greene, George W. *The Life of Nathanael Greene, Major-General in the Army of the Revolution.* 3 vols. Freeport, NY: Books for Libraries Press, 1972.

Hall, Verna M. *The Christian History of the Constitution of the United States of America.* San Francisco: Foundation for American Christian Education, 1983.

Hanna, Willard A. *The Berkshire–Litchfield Legacy.* C. E. Tuttle and Company, 1984.

Harrison, Lowell H. *George Rogers Clark and the War in the West.* Lexington, KY: University of Kentucky Press, 2001.

Hatch, Robert McConnell. *Major John Andre: A Gallant in Spy's Clothing.* New York: Houghton Mifflin, 1986.

Haugen, Brenda. *Martha Washington: First Lady of the United States.* Compass Point Books, 2005.

Haw, James. " 'Every Thing Here Depends upon Opinion': Nathanael Greene and Public Support in the Southern Campaigns of the American Revolution." *South Carolina Historical Magazine,* 109 (July 2008): 212-31.

Heinemann, Ronald L., John G. Kolp, Anthony S. Parent, Jr., and William G. Shade. *Old Dominion, New Commonwealth: A History of Virginia, 1607-2007.* University of Virginia Press, 2007.

Hibbert, Christopher. *Redcoats and Rebels: The War for America 1770-1781.* Grafton Books, 1990

Hobson, Charles F. and Robert A. Rutlands, eds. *The Papers of James Madison: Volume 12, 2 March 1789-20 January 1790.* Charlottesville: University Press of Virginia, 1979.

Hogeland, William. *Declaration: The Nine Tumultuous Weeks When America Became Independent, May 1–July 4, 1776.* New York: Simon & Schuster, 2010.

Hutchinson, Francis. *A Fair Account of the Late Unhappy Disturbance at Boston.* London: B. White, 1770.

Isaacson, Walter. *Benjamin Franklin: An American Life.* New York: Simon & Schuster, 2004.

Jefferson, Thomas. *Jefferson's "Bible"; The Life and Morals of Jesus of Nazareth XV-XVI.* ed. Judd Patton (Grove City): American Book Distributors, 1996.

Jefferson, Thomas. *The Writings of Thomas Jefferson, Vol. 9.* ed. Paul Leicester Ford. New York: G.P. Putnam's Sons, 1899.

Johnson, Clifton (1915). *The Picturesque Hudson.* MacMillan. Retrieved 2009-07-08.

Jones, Charles Colcock. *Sergeant William Jasper.* Kessinger Publishing, 2010

Kaplan, Sidney, and Emma Nogrady Kaplan. *The Black Presence in the Era of the American Revolution.* Amherst, MA: The University of Massachusetts Press, 1989.

Ketcham, Ralph Louis. *James Madison: A Biography.* Charlottesville, VA: University of Virginia Press, 1971.

Ketchum, Richard M. *Saratoga: Turning Point of America's Revolutionary War.* New York: Henry Holt, 1997.

Kopperman, Paul. *Braddock at the Monongahela.* Pittsburgh, PA: University of Pittsburgh Press, 1977.

Krensky, Stephen. *DK Biography: Benjamin Franklin.* DK Children, 2007.

Labunski, Richard. *James Madison and the Struggle for the Bill of Rights.* New York, NY: Oxford University Press, 2006.

Lane, Jason. *General and Madame de Lafayette: Partners in Liberty's Cause in the American and French Revolutions.* Taylor Trade Publishing, 2003.

Lindenmeyer, Otto. *Black & Brave: The Black Soldier in America.* New York, 1970.

Loane, Nancy K. *Following the Drum: Women at the Valley Forge Encampment.* Potomac Books, Inc., 2009.

Lockhart, Paul Douglas. *The Drillmaster of Valley Forge: the Baron de Von Steuben and the Making of the American Army.* New York: Harper Collins, 2008.

Lodge, Henry Cabot and Theodore Roosevelt. *Hero Tales from American History,* George Grant, ed. White Hall, WV: Tolle Lege Press, 2012.

Luzader, John F. *Saratoga: A Military History of the Decisive Campaign of the American Revolution.* New York: Savas Beatie, 2010.

Maier, Pauline. *American Scripture: Making the Declaration of Independence.* New York: Knopf, 1997.

Marshall, Peter and David Manuel. *The Light and the Glory.* Revell, 1977.

Martin, James Kirby. *Benedict Arnold, Revolutionary War Hero: An American Warrior Reconsidered.* New York: New York University Press, 1997.

Massachusetts Historical Society. *Henry Knox Diary, 20 November 1775 to 13 January 1776.*

Massey, Gregory D. *General Nathanael Greene and the American Revolution in the South.* University of South Carolina Press, 2012.

McClung, Robert. *Young George Washington and the French and Indian War, 1753-1758.* Linnet Books, 2002.

McCrady, Edward. *The History of South Carolina in the Revolution, 1775-1780.* New York: Macmillan, 1901.

McCullough, David. *1776.* New York: Simon & Schuster, 2005.

Messick, Hank. *King's Mountain: The Epic of the Blue Ridge "Mountain Men" in the American Revolution.* New York: Little & Brown, 1976.

Middlekauff, Robert. *The Glorious Cause: The American Revolution, 1763-1789.* New York and Oxford: Oxford University Press, 2007.

Milgrim, Shirley Gorson. *Haym Salomon: Liberty's Son.* The Jewish Publication Society, 1979.

Mintz, Max M. *The Generals of Saratoga: John Burgoyne and Horatio Gates.* New Haven, CT: Yale University Press, 1990.

Morrissey, Brendan. *Saratoga 1777: Turning Point of a Revolution.* Oxford: Osprey Publishing, 2000.

Morrill, Dan. *Southern Campaigns of the American Revolution.* Nautical & Aviation Publishing, 1993.

National Archives Education Staff. *The Constitution: Evolution of a Government.* Santa Barbara: ABC-CLIO, Inc., 2001.

Pancake, John. *This Destructive War.* University of Alabama Press, 1985.

Payan, Gregory. *Marquis de Lafayette: French Hero of the American Revolution.* The Rosen Publishing Group, 2002.

Peacock, Louise. *Crossing the Delaware: A History in Many Voices.* Aladdin, 2007.

Peters, Madison C. *Haym Salomon: The Financier of the Revolution.* University Press of the Pacific, 2005.

Puls, Mark. *Henry Knox: Visionary General of the American Revolution.* New York: Palgrave, 2010.

Randall, Henry Stephens. *The Life of Thomas Jefferson,* Vol. 3. New York: Derby & Jackson, 1858.

Randall, William Sterne. *Benedict Arnold: Patriot and Traitor.* Dorset Press, 2001.

Randall, Williard Sterne. *Ethan Allen: His Life and Times.* New York: W. W. Norton, 2011.

Reit, Seymour. *Guns for General Washington: A Story of the American Revolution.* Sandpiper, 2001.

Rosen, Gary. *American Compact: James Madison and the Problem of Founding.* Lawrence, KS: University Press of Kansas, 1999.

Russell, Charles Edward. *Haym Solomon and the Revolution.* Ayer Company Publishers, 1930.

Rutland, Robert Allen. *James Madison: The Founding Father.* Columbia, MO: University of Missouri Press, 1987.

Saillant, John. *Black Puritan, Black Republican: The Life and Thought of Lemuel Haynes, 1753-1833.* New York: Oxford University Press, 2003.

Savas, Theodore P., and Dameron, J. David. *A Guide to the Battles of the American Revolution.* Savas Beatie, 2005.

Scheer, George F. and Hugh F. Rankin, *Rebels and Redcoats.* New York: The World Publishing Company, 1957.

Schwartz, Laurens R. *Jews and the American Revolution: Haym Solomon and Others,* Jefferson, NC: McFarland & Co., 1987.

Scollay, Mercy to Elijah Dix. "I Wear a Face Foreign to the Feelings of My Heart" (Boston: April 26, 1776). *Mercy Scollay Papers, 1775-1824.* Cambridge, MA: Cambridge Historical Society.

Silverman, Jerry. *Of Thee I Sing.* Citadel Press, 2002.

Silvey, Anita. *Henry Knox: Bookseller, Soldier, Patriot.* Clarion Books, 2010.

Simpson, Andrew. "In St. Patrick's Shadow: The Peculiar Holiday of Evacuation Day," *The Bostonian Society News* (2004, Issue 1).

Steele, William O. *John Sevier: Pioneer Boy. The Childhood of Famous Americans Series.* Indianapolis: Bobbs-Merrill, 1953.

Stewart, David O. *The Summer of 1787: The Men Who Invented the Constitution.* New York: Simon & Schuster, 2008.

Sumner Letter, "Boston 1775," accessed on 02/08/2013.

Tonsetic, Robert. *1781: The Decisive Year of the Revolutionary War.* Casemate, 2011.

Uhlar, Janet. *Liberty's Martyr: The Story of Dr. Joseph Warren.* Dog Ear Publishing, 2009.

Unger, Harlow Giles. *Lafayette.* Hoboken, NJ: John Wiley & Sons, 2002.

Vile, John R. *The Constitutional Convention of 1787: A Comprehensive Encyclopedia of America's Founding.* 2 Vols. ABC-CLIO: 2005.

Walett, Francis. "James Bowdoin, Patriot Propagandist." *The New England Quarterly:* 23:3 (September 1950).

Ware, Susan. *Forgotten Heroes: Inspiring American Portraits from Our Leading Historians.* Portland, OR: Simon & Schuster, 2000.

Warren, Joseph. *The Suffolk Resolves,* September 9, 1774.

Washington, George to Martha Washington, "My Dearest Life and Love," June 24, 1776.

Washington, George to William Gordon. "8 July 1788." *Writings,* 27: 49-52.

Wheeler, Richard "Little Bear." *God's Mighty Hand: Providential Occurrences in World History,* Bulverde, TX: Mantle Ministries Press.

Wheeler, William Bruce, Susan Becker, and Lorri Glover. *Discovering the American Past: A Look at the Evidence: To 1877.* Belmont, CA: Cengage Learning, 2011.

White, Alain C. *The History of the Town of Litchfield, Connecticut, 1720-1920.* Litchfield, CT: Enquirer Print, 1920.

White, Richard. *Jordan Freeman Was My Friend.* Xlibris Corps, 2003 (Historical Fiction).

Wilson, Barry K. *Benedict Arnold: A Traitor in Our Midst.* McGill Queens Press, 2001.

York, Neil Longley. *The Boston Massacre: A History with Documents.* New York: Taylor & Francis, 2010.

Websites and Other Media

Brennan, Daniel. "Did James Madison suffer a nervous collapse due to the intensity of his studies?" Mudd Manuscript Library Blog, January 2008, Princeton University Archives and Public Policy Papers Collection, Princeton University.

Fowler, William M. "Glover, John." *American National Biography Online,* www.anb.org/ February 2000.

Garden, Alexander. *"Sergeant Jasper, 2nd Regiment." Anecdotes of the Revolutionary War in America. 1822.* http://books.google.com/books?id=WJ98ynQ-W-AC&pg=PA90

"Henry Knox and the 'Noble Train of Artillery' " on the *Fort Ticonderoga National Historic Landmark* http://www.fort-ticonderoga.org/history/bibliographies/henry_knox.htm

"Heralds of a Liberal Faith," Volumes I-IV. http://harvardsquarelibrary.org/Heralds/Jonathan-Mayhew.php

Sevier, William Jay, and Lance Sevier. "The Life of John Sevier Time Line, Including Family Origins & World Events, 1506 -1815." http://www.johnsevier.com/jstime.html

"Saratoga National Historical Park." National Park Service. http://www.nps.gov/sara/.

(Documentary DVD) *Von Steuben's Continentals: The First American Army* (Actor: John D. Pagano, Lionheart Filmworks, 2007).

Photo Credits

Availability

Drawing of General Nathanael Greene: http://www.tumblr.com/tagged/nathanael%20greene

Woman on horseback: 960829-clipart.com

Woman on horse in river: 267617-clipart.com

Cautiousness

James Armistead: Public domain. http://publicdomainclipart.blogspot.com/2012/02/james-armistead-lafayette.html

Courage

Plaque: Public Domain. http://www.negroartist.com/REVOLUTIONAY%20WAR/images/JORDAN%20FREEMAN1_jpg.jpg

British landing at Groton: http://jhasara.blogspot.com/2012/04/death-of-colonel-ledyard-at-battle-of.html

Battle of Fort Griswold: Groton City Hall, http://jhasara.blogspot.com/2012/04/death-of-colonel-ledyard-at-battle-of.html, painting by David Wagner

Decisiveness

Daniel Morgan Portrait: Public Domain. http://en.wikipedia.org/wiki/File:DanielMorgan.jpeg

Battle of Cowpens: www.Army.mil: http://usarmy.vo.llnwd.net/e2/-images/2008/01/13/11938/army.mil-2008-03-26-145626.jpg, painting by Don Troiani for the National Guard Bureau Heritage Series

Discernment

Alexis de Tocqueville: Public Domain. http://en.wikipedia.org/wiki/File:Alexis_de_tocqueville.jpg

Generosity

Haym Solomon Portrait: Public Domain. National Archives and Records Administration, http://en.wikipedia.org/wiki/File:Salomon,_Haym_%28bust%29_-_NARA_-_532941.jpg

Signing paperwork: http://www.nps.gov/revwar/images/about_the_rev/haym_solomon2.jpg

Statue-Chicago: Heald Square Monument: http://en.wikipedia.org/wiki/File:Heald_Monument_%282%29.JPG, TonyTheTiger at en.wikipedia

Prudence

Independence Hall interior: http://jfkplusfifty.files.wordpress.com/2011/05/independence_hall_assembly_room.jpg

Benjamin Franklin Portrait: Public Domain. http://ushistory-images.com/benjamin-franklin.shtm

President's chair Independence Hall: photograph. http://www.nps.gov/inde/independence-hall-1.htm

Purposefulness

Star Fort: http://minerdescent.com/2012/07/04/carolina-in-the-revolution/

General Nathanael Green Portrait: Public Domain. http://clio.missouristate.edu/FTMiller/LocalHistory/Portraits/rev080Greene%20%281%29.jpg

Portrait of Thaddeus Kosciuszko: Public Domain. http://en.wikipedia.org/wiki/File:Tadeusz_Ko%C5%9Bciuszko.PNG

Portrait of Col. Cruger: Public Domain. http://www.nps.gov/nisi/historyculture/images/Cruger_web.jpg

Maham Tower: http://www.nps.gov/nisi/parknews/images/Maham_tower_firing_fixed_web.jpg

Siege of Ninety-Six: http://www.revolutionaryday.com/usroute221/ninetysix/default.htm

Thoroughness

James Madison Portrait: Public Domain. http://ushistoryimages.com/president-madison.shtm

Constitution: http://billofrightsinstitute.org/blog/2011/09/12/ways-to-celebrate-constitution-day/

Signing of Constitution: Public Domain. U.S. Capitol, http://www.aoc.gov/capitol-hill/murals/signing-constitution

Uprightness

Thomas Jefferson Portrait: Public Domain. State Room portrait by Charles Willson Peale, 1790's

"Jefferson Bible" cutouts: http://newsdesk.si.edu/photos/jefferson-bible-source-bible; photo by Hugh Talman, Smithsonian's National Museum of American History

Jefferson Bible title page: http://theodecorte.files.wordpress.com/2012/07/0470.jpeg

Endnotes

[1]David Barton, *Spirit of the American Revolution*, quoting de Tocqueville, "The Republic of the United States of America and Its Political Institutions, Reviewed and Examined," Henry Reeves, translator (New York: A.S. Barnes & Co. 1851), Vol. I, p.337

About the Authors

Marilyn Boyer is the mother of fourteen children, all home schooled from kindergarten through high school. Her passion to train up her children in the character of Christ led her to create Character Concepts Curriculum, a character curriculum for kids of all ages to equip parents in raising children of integrity!

Her many character resources, as well as books on homeschooling and Christian parenting, are available online.

About the Authors

Grace Tumas Ehrman holds a degree in history from Liberty University. Her paper, "Warlords and Samurais: Japanese Interventionists in Siberia During the Russian Civil War, 1918-1922," won an award at the 2013 Phi Alpha Theta History Conference. She specializes in American and Russian history.

LEGENDS of FAITH
Early Church FATHERS
Early Church FATHERS
Marilyn Boyer
BOYER
ISBN 13: 978-1-68344-400-8
LEGENDS of FAITH
MISSIONARIES for Christ
MISSIONARIES for Christ
Marilyn Boyer
BOYER
ISBN 13: 978-1-68344-402-2
LEGENDS of FAITH
Famous PREACHERS and EVANGELISTS
Marilyn Boyer
ISBN 13: 978-1-68344-401-5
LEGENDS of FAITH
Famous HYMNWRITERS
Famous HYMNWRITERS
Marilyn Boyer
BOYER
ISBN 13: 978-1-68344-403-9